Active Korean 1

Active Korean 1

서울대학교 언어교육원
Language Education Institute
Seoul National University

TWO PONDS
|주| 투판즈

Preface 머리말

Active Korean 1은 한국어 성인 학습자를 위한 단기 연수용(약 60시간) 한국어 교재 시리즈 중 첫째 권이다. 그동안 대부분의 한국어 교재는 집중 과정용으로 개발되어, 단기간에 실제적인 한국어 의사소통 능력을 키우고자 하는 학습자에게는 비효율적인 측면이 있었다. 이 책은 한국어를 처음 배우는 학습자들이 단기간에 기초적인 의사소통 능력을 갖추도록 하기 위해서 개발되었으며, 다음과 같은 특징을 가지고 있다.

첫째, 상황 및 기능 중심적 교수요목을 바탕으로 일상생활에서 사용하는 실제적이고 기본적인 내용으로 구성하였다. 초급 학습자들에게 필수적인 상황 및 기능을 중심으로 어휘와 문법, 표현을 선정하였다.

둘째, 체계적인 어휘 및 문법 학습이 이루어지도록 하였다. 매 과의 첫머리에 의미 범주와 품사별로 어휘 목록을 제시하고, 매 과의 마지막에 확장 표현 및 어휘를 제시하여 학습의 편의를 꾀하였다. 또한 문법 항목에 대한 자세한 설명을 통해 학습자가 문법을 정확하게 이해하여 적절하게 사용할 수 있도록 하였다.

셋째, 의사소통 기능을 통합적으로 활용하고 목표 문법을 완전히 습득하도록 하는 과제와 활동을 다양하게 제공하였다. 이러한 과제 수행을 통해 학습자는 유창성을 향상시키고 학습 의욕을 고취시킬 수 있다.

넷째, 수업의 구조와 학습자를 고려하여 단원 체제를 구성하였다. 주제와 상황에 맞는 문법과 표현, 그것을 활용한 간단한 대화, 확장된 담화의 순으로 제시함으로써 수업의 일반적 구조에 맞고 학습자의 이해와 활용이 용이하게 하였다.

다섯째, 본 교재에서는 어휘와 표현, 문법과 함께 듣기, 말하기, 읽기, 쓰기를 통합적으로 활용할 수 있는 능력을 기른다. 별도로 구성된 워크북을 통해서는 어휘 및 표현 연습과 문법 연습을 통해 학습 내용을 연습하고 정리해 볼 수 있다.

여섯째, 다양한 사진과 삽화 등 시각 자료를 풍부하게 제공하여 실제적이고 흥미 있는 학습이 가능하도록 하였다. 또한 시각 자료를 통해 의미와 상황을 정확하게 전달하고 학습자의 흥미를 유발함으로써 학습 효과를 높이고자 하였다.

일곱째, 수업용 교재로서뿐만 아니라 자율 학습용 교재로서도 사용이 가능하도록 배려하였다. 각 과에 제시된 순서대로 학습해 나가면 성공적인 학습 결과를 얻을 수 있도록 구성하였으며, 문법 설명과 지시문 등이 영어로 명료하게 제시되어 있다. 또한 학습 결과를 스스로 점검하고 확인할 수 있어 자기 평가가 가능하다.

이 책이 완성되기까지 오랜 기간에 걸쳐 집필 및 출판 과정에 헌신적으로 참여해 주신 교재개발위원회 선생님들, 번역을 맡아 주신 한국어교육센터의 함창덕 선생님, 현혜미 선생님, 번역 감수를 해 주신 외국어교육센터의 박준성 선생님의 노고에 이 자리를 빌려 깊은 감사를 드린다. 아울러 이 책이 출판되기까지 많은 도움을 주신 투판즈의 사장님과 편집진 여러분께도 감사의 마음을 전한다.

2006. 6.

장 소 원

서울대학교 언어교육원 한국어교육센터 소장

Active Korean 1 is the first volume in the Korean language textbook series designed for adult learners in a short-term training course (about 60 hours) of Korean language. Most textbooks of Korean language up until recently were developed for intensive courses, so they were not suitable for learners who wanted to improve their communication skills in a short period of time. Written for adult learners who are beginning to learn Korean as a foreign language, it aims to develop learners' basic communication skills in a short period of time by using the following methods:

First, on the basis of a situation and function centered syllabus, this book is composed of essential vocabulary, grammar and expressions for beginners derived from everyday situations and functions of real-life.

Second, this book aims to enable learners to acquire vocabulary and grammar systematically. To facilitate active vocabulary building, vocabulary lists, which are categorized by meanings and parts of speech, are presented on the first page of each unit, and extended vocabulary and expressions are presented at the end of each unit. Through the detailed explanation of grammar items, learners are able to understand the target grammar accurately and use it appropriately.

Third, various tasks and activities are provided to enable learners to acquire the target grammar and apply it to practical situations. Through these challenging tasks and activities, learners are able to improve their communicative competence.

Fourth, units are organized in consideration of class structure and learners. Grammar and expressions related to the topic and the given situations, a simple dialogue based on the topic and an extended conversation are presented in order in every unit to suit a general class structure and to facilitate learners' understanding and application.

Fifth, this book features integration of vocabulary, expressions, grammar, listening, speaking, reading and writing. The separate workbook helps learners to practice and organize what they have learned from the main textbook through exercises in grammar, expressions and vocabulary.

Sixth, a wide variety of photos and illustrations are provided to arouse learners' interests in learning and enable learners to have an accurate understanding of the given meanings and situations.

Seventh, this book can be used not only as a textbook for classes but also as a self-study book. Studying each unit in order will lead learners to successfully learn on one's own. To facilitate learners' understanding, explanations on grammar and instructions are presented in English, and self-assessment is possible as well.

We wish to express our sincere gratitude to all the instructors from the Textbook Development Committee who have contributed to the work of writing and publication of this book. We are also greatly indebted to Mr. Chang-Deok Hahm and Hae-mi Hyun from the Korean Language Education Center for editing the English translations, Mr. Joon-Sung Park from the Foreign Language Education Center for proofreading the translations. In addition, we would like to convey our gratitude to the CEO of TWOPONDS and his editorial staff for their generous support in having this volume published.

June 2006

So-Wonne Tchang

Director, Korean Language Education Center
Language Education Institute, Seoul National University

How to Use This Book 일러두기

This book consists of 9 units. Unit 1 is a preliminary lesson for Hangeul (Korean alphabet) which consists of an introduction of Hangeul and exercises. The other 8 units consist of the following sections.

In This Unit

Objectives and functions to learn in each unit are presented in 'In This Unit.'

Expressions

The key expressions related to the topic and functions of each unit are presented in this section. These essential expressions for communication are presented in sentence unit.

Vocabulary

New vocabulary words that appear in each unit are presented in this section. Collocational expressions are categorized separately by 'Words that go together.' This 'Vocabulary' section will function as a dictionary for learners while studying each unit.

Key Dialogues 핵심 대화

Ordering at a restaurant (1)

Grammar Points

V-(으)세요

A 어서 오세요. 뭐 드릴까요?

B 불고기 주세요.

A Welcome. What would you like to have?

B I'd like to have bulgogi.

Notes

Grammar Points

N 주세요

Practice

1. Change the words below as shown in the example.

가다 → 가세요

1) 오다 →　2) 읽다 →

3) 앉다 →　4) 기다리다 →

2. You are at a restaurant. Order the following food.

1) 냉면　2) 비빔밥

3) 라면　4) 김밥

52 UNIT 3

Key Dialogues

This section introduces a few sets of a short dialogue and the grammar points.

Grammar Points

Key explanations on the new grammar points of each unit are presented. More explanations on the grammar are presented in 'Grammar Reference' at the end of this book.

Notes

Basic explanations on the essential vocabulary and expressions used in the conversation are presented.

Practice

You can review what you have learned in 'Grammar Points' through various forms of exercises. The answers are presented upside down on the same page.

Conversation Drills 대화 연습

Conversation 1

A 안녕하세요?

B 안녕하세요? 저는 크리스예요.

A 크리스 씨는 미국 사람이에요?

B 아니요, 저는 호주 사람이에요.

A 크리스 씨는 선생님이에요?

B 네, 저는 선생님이에요.

Check it

Practice the dialogue with your partner.

42 UNIT 2

Conversation Drills

A couple of longer dialogues designed to allow learners to practice the sentences from 'Key Dialogues' are presented in this section. Role play using the drills at the bottom allows learners to practice the dialogue.

Check it

'Check it' enhances learners' comprehension of the dialogue.

How to Use This Book 일러두기

Tasks & Activites 과제

1. Pair work

Look at the ID cards below, then ask questions about them to your partner.

외국인등록증 871019-6300291 Chen Wei China

외국인등록증 760420-6836781 Bevoll Anna Maria Germany

외국인등록증 830107-5933018 William Robert The United States of America

외국인등록증 851230-5987561 Ito Yoshio Japan

이름이 뭐예요?

첸웨이예요.

한국 사람이에요?

아니요, 중국 사람이에요.

44 UNIT 2

Tasks & Activities

Various tasks and activities in this section such as interviews and games are related to the topic and functions of each unit, and these tasks and activities make each lesson task-based and significant.

Listening 듣기

TRACK 09

1. Listen carefully, and choose the correct picture.

1) ① 선생님 ② 학생 ③ 회사원

2) ① 캐나다 ② 한국 ③ 러시아

2. Listen carefully, and choose the picture that best fits the dialogue.

① ② ③

46 UNIT 2

Listening

This is a listening exercise covering grammar, vocabulary and expressions that are carried throughout each unit. The dialogue in this section is using authentic language in a wide range of settings to help learners prepare for real-life listening tasks.

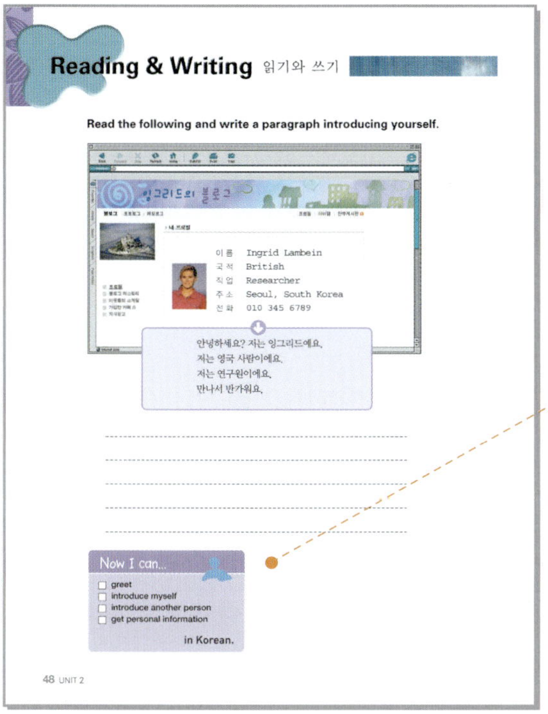

Reading & Writing

This section provides reading and writing practices through read-and-answer and read-and-write exercises to help learners understand the written language and improve their written expressions.

Now I can

Each unit ends with the opportunity for learners to wrap up what they have learned and assess their achievement of learning objectives.

Additional Expressions

Extended vocabulary words and expressions are presented with illustrations and photos. Although they are a little beyond the level of each unit, they are useful expressions for daily life.

How to Use This Book 일러두기

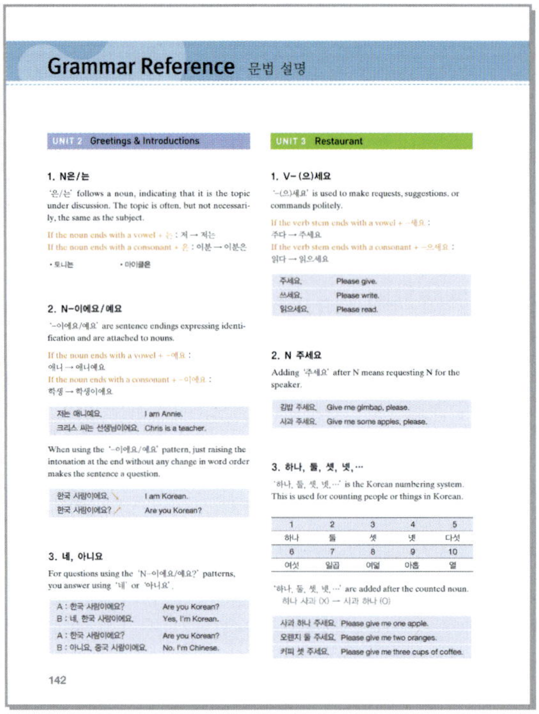

Grammar Reference

This section at the end of the book presents detailed explanations of 'Grammar Points' in each unit. Further explanations on grammar structures will be helpful for learners as well as instructors.

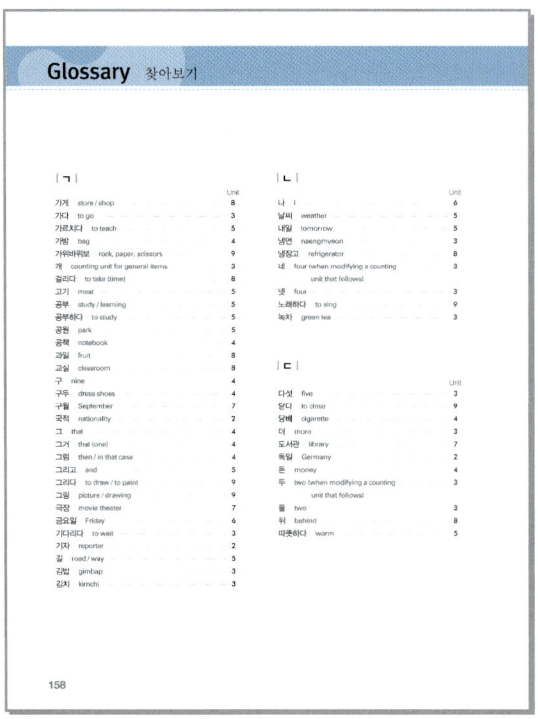

Glossary

It lists all the vocabulary words presented throughout the textbook and Grammar Reference with the meanings, and indicates the unit where they first appear.

Abbreviations in the book

N	noun	A	adjective
V	verb	S	sentence

Contents 차례

Scope and Sequence 교재 구성표

Unit	Expressions 표현	Vocabulary 어휘	Grammar 문법	Key Dialogues 핵심 대화
Unit 1 Hangeul 한글	• Introduction to Hangeul • Consonants and Vowels • Hangeul (1) - Reading / Writing / Listening • Hangeul (2) - Reading / Writing / Listening		• Hangeul (3) - Reading / Writing / Listening • Hangeul (4) - Reading / Writing / Listening • Hangeul (5) - Reading / Writing / Listening	
Unit 2 Greetings & Introductions 인사와 소개	• Expressions related to greetings and introductions	• Countries • Occupations	• N은/는 • N–이에요/예요 • 네, 아니요	• Greetings • Introducing yourself • Introducing another person • Getting personal information
Unit 3 Restaurant 식당	• Expressions used at restaurants	• Food • Drinks • Numbers • Counting units	• V–(으)세요 • N 주세요 • 하나, 둘, 셋, 넷,… • 병, 개, 잔 • N하고 N′	• Ordering at a restaurant • Asking for more
Unit 4 Shopping 쇼핑	• Expressions related to shopping	• Demonstratives • Numbers	• N이/가 있어요/없어요 • 이거, 그거, 저거 • 이 N, 그 N, 저 N • 일, 이, 삼, 사,…	• Asking if someone has an item • Asking the name of things with demonstratives • Describing things with demonstratives • Asking prices
Unit 5 Daily Life 일상생활	• Questions related to daily life	• Places • Time • Food • Interrogatives	• A/V–아요/어요 • N을/를 • N에 가다/오다 • 안 A/V • N이/가 A • 그리고	• Talking about daily life • Expressing movement • Expressing negation • Describing a person or a thing • Linking two sentences

Conversation Drills 대화 연습	Tasks & Activities 과제	Listening 듣기	Reading & Writing 읽기와 쓰기	Additional Expressions 추가 표현
• Obtaining personal information • Introducing two people to each other	• Exchanging personal information	• Listening to greetings • Listening for personal information	• About myself (name, nationality, occupation, etc.)	• Vocabulary related to occupations
• Ordering at a restaurant	• Ordering food as directed	• Listening for what has been ordered • Listening to imperative expressions	• Ordering food	• Vocabulary related to food and tableware
• Buying items at a store	• Selling and buying items	• Listening for prices • Listening for items purchased	• Buying an item at a store	• Counting units for various items
• Talking about today's schedule • One's likes and dislikes	• Getting information about someone	• Listening for different tastes in food • Listening to one's daily schedule	• About my friends	• Daily life expressions

Scope and Sequence 교재 구성표

Unit	Expressions 표현	Vocabulary 어휘	Grammar 문법	Key Dialogues 핵심 대화
Unit 6 Time 시간	• Expressions related to time and days of the week	• Time • Days of the week • Interrogatives	• __시 __분 • 요일 • N에 • S-지만 S′	• Telling time • Expressing days of the week • Telling the time when something happens • Expressing contrast
Unit 7 Appointment 약속	• Expressions related to suggestions	• Months • Time • Places	• V-(으)ㄹ까요? • __월 __일 • A/V-았어요 / 었어요 • N에서	• Making suggestions • Giving the date • Talking about something you did in the past • Talking about places
Unit 8 Locations & Directions 위치와 방향	• Expressions on places and directions	• Locations / Positions • Places • Furniture & Home appliances	• N이/가 N′에 있다/없다 • N 위/아래/앞/뒤/옆/안에 • N(으)로 가다/오다 • N까지 • 분, 시간	• Asking whether an item exists or not • Giving the location of an item • Asking for and giving locations • Asking for and giving directions • Asking how long it takes to the destination
Unit 9 Phone Call 전화	• Expressions related to phone calls	• Vocabulary related to phone calls	• N-(이)지요? • V-아/어 주세요 • V-고 있다	• Asking if you called the right number • Putting someone on the phone • Expressing an action in progress

Conversation Drills 대화 연습	Tasks & Activities 과제	Listening 듣기	Reading & Writing 읽기와 쓰기	Additional Expressions 추가 표현
• Talking about daily schedules	• Talking about daily routines	• Listening to hourly activities • Listening to daily activities • Listening to one's daily schedule	• My daily schedule	• Words which indicate time
• Making follow-up suggestions • Making an appointment	• Making appointments according to the schedule	• Listening for the date • Figuring out the date • Listening for appointments	• What I did yesterday	• Places
• Asking for and giving locations • Asking for and giving directions	• Getting information about locations	• Listening for locations	• About my room	• Important expressions for giving directions
• Making a phone call	• Making requests	• Listening to over the phone conversations • Listening for requests	• Understanding what people are doing • Leaving a telephone message	• Additional expressions related to phone numbers • Additional expressions related to telephone conversations • Useful phone numbers in Korea

UNIT 1

Hangeul

한글

In This Unit

- Introduction to Hangeul 한글에 대한 소개
- Learning the vowels of Hangeul 한글 모음 익히기
- Learning the consonants of Hangeul 한글 자음 익히기

Introduction to Hangeul

Korean uses its own unique alphabet called Hangeul. It is considered to be one of the most efficient alphabets in the world and has garnered unanimous praise from language experts for its scientific design and excellence.

Hangeul was created under King Sejong during the Joseon Dynasty (1393 -1910). In 1446, the first Korean alphabet was proclaimed under the original name Hun-min-jeong-eum, which literally meant 'the correct sounds for the instruction of the people.'

Hangeul consists of 14 consonants and 10 vowels, totaling 24 basic characters. The shapes of Hangeul's consonants were formed after voice organs (such as lip, tongue, throat, etc.) while those of the vowels were formed after what one might say symbolizes heaven, earth, and human beings.

All words in Korean are composed of syllables, which go by the following basic rules:

1. A syllable begins with a consonant.
2. A syllable has at least one consonant and one vowel.
3. Each syllable gets written in a square box.

A syllable that consists of a consonant and a 'vertical vowel' is written with the consonant on the left and the vowel on the right.

ㄴ [n] + ㅏ [a] = 나 [na]

A syllable that consists of a consonant and a 'horizontal vowel' is written with the consonant on top and the vowel underneath.

ㄴ [n] + ㅗ [o] = 노 [no]

If a syllable shows a consonant-vowel-consonant combination, in other words, if a syllable ends with a consonant, called batchim (meaning 'supporting floor' in Korean), the final consonant goes to the bottom – or floor – of that syllable.

ㅁ [m] + ㅏ [a] + ㄴ [n] = 만 [man]
ㅁ [m] + ㅗ [o] + ㄱ [k] = 목 [mok]

All symbols of Hangeul are written from top to bottom and from left to right. Strokes are never interrupted, not even when they change directions halfway.

Consonants and Vowels

Consonants

Letter	ㄱ	ㄴ	ㄷ	ㄹ	ㅁ	ㅂ	ㅅ	ㅇ	ㅈ	ㅎ
Sound Value	[k/g]	[n]	[t/d]	[r/l]	[m]	[p/b]	[s]	[ø/ŋ]	[tʃ/j]	[h]
Letter	ㅋ		ㅌ			ㅍ			ㅊ	
Sound Value	[kʰ]		[tʰ]			[pʰ]			[tʃʰ]	
Letter	ㄲ		ㄸ			ㅃ	ㅆ		ㅉ	
Sound Value	[k']		[t']			[p']	[s']		[tʃ']	

Vowels

Letter	ㅏ	ㅓ	ㅗ	ㅜ	ㅡ	ㅣ	ㅔ	ㅐ	ㅚ	ㅟ
Sound Value	[a]	[ə]	[o]	[u]	[ɨ]	[i]	[e]	[ɛ]	[ö/we]	[ü/wi]
Letter	ㅑ	ㅕ	ㅛ	ㅠ			ㅖ	ㅒ		
Sound Value	[ya]	[yə]	[yo]	[yu]			[ye]	[yɛ]		
Letter	ㅘ	ㅝ			ㅢ		ㅞ	ㅙ		
Sound Value	[wa]	[wə]			[ɨy]		[we]	[wɛ]		

Hangeul

Here are some basic Hangeul syllables.

가	갸	거	겨	고	교	구	규	그	기
나	냐	너	녀	노	뇨	누	뉴	느	니
다	댜	더	뎌	도	됴	두	듀	드	디
라	랴	러	려	로	료	루	류	르	리
마	먀	머	며	모	묘	무	뮤	므	미
바	뱌	버	벼	보	뵤	부	뷰	브	비
사	샤	서	셔	소	쇼	수	슈	스	시
아	야	어	여	오	요	우	유	으	이
자	쟈	저	져	조	죠	주	쥬	즈	지
차	챠	처	쳐	초	쵸	추	츄	츠	치
카	캬	커	켜	코	쿄	쿠	큐	크	키
타	탸	터	텨	토	툐	투	튜	트	티
파	퍄	퍼	펴	포	표	푸	퓨	프	피
하	햐	허	혀	호	효	후	휴	흐	히

Hangeul (1)

Those vowels having longer vertical strokes will always carry consonants on the left of it while horizontal vowels carry them on top.

No Korean vowels can stand alone at the beginning of a Korean syllable without a preceding consonant, but if it has no consonant sound value of its own, it must be preceded by the consonant ‘ㅇ’, which is silent when positioned at the beginning of a syllable.

Letter	ㅏ	ㅑ	ㅓ	ㅕ	ㅗ	ㅛ	ㅜ	ㅠ	ㅡ	ㅣ
Sound Value	[a]	[ya]	[ə]	[yə]	[o]	[yo]	[u]	[yu]	[ɨ]	[i]
Writing Order	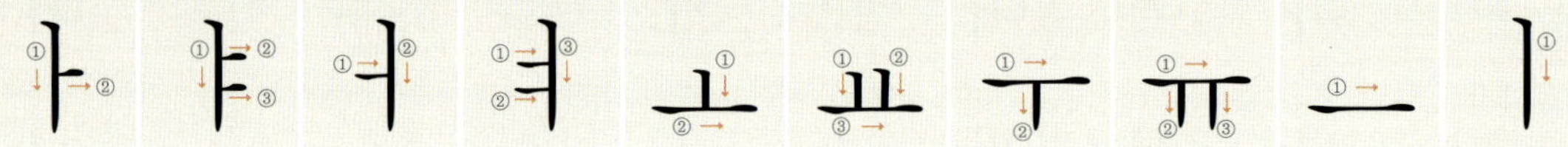									

● Listen to the following. TRACK 02

아　야　어　여　오　요　우　유　으　이

● Read the following words.

아이

오이

우유

여우

Write the following words.

아	이	아	이				
오	이	오	이				
우	유	우	유				
여	우	여	우				

Exercise

TRACK 02

1. Listen carefully, and choose the correct syllable.

1) ① 어 ② 아
2) ① 여 ② 유
3) ① 오 ② 우
4) ① 야 ② 유
5) ① 으 ② 이

2. Listen carefully, and number the words as you listen.

[1)] 이	☐ 유아	☐ 오이
☐ 우아	☐ 여유	☐ 우유

Answer **1.** 1) ② 2) ① 3) ① 4) ② 5) ① **2.** 1) 이 2) 우유 3) 오이 4) 유아 5) 여유

Hangeul (2)

Consonants cannot be used alone. It should be combined with a vowel to form a syllable.

Letter	ㄱ	ㄴ	ㄷ	ㄹ	ㅁ	ㅂ	ㅅ	ㅇ	ㅈ	ㅎ
Sound Value	[k/g]	[n]	[t/d]	[r/l]	[m]	[p/b]	[s]	[ø]	[tʃ/j]	[h]
Writing Order	ㄱ	ㄴ	ㄷ	ㄹ	ㅁ	ㅂ	ㅅ	ㅇ	ㅈ	ㅎ

Listen to the following. TRACK 03

가 나 다 라 마 바 사 아 자 하

Read the following words.

가구

나무

구두

라디오

바나나

가수

아기

바지

호수

Write the following words.

가구	가구		
나무	나무		
구두	구두		
라디오	라디오		
바나나	바나나		
가수	가수		
아기	아기		
바지	바지		
호수	호수		

Exercise

TRACK 03

1. Listen carefully, and choose the correct syllable.

1) ① 가 ② 다
2) ① 마 ② 나
3) ① 아 ② 라
4) ① 자 ② 바
5) ① 하 ② 사

2. Listen carefully, and number the words as you listen.

[1)] 아기　[ ] 허리　[ ] 노루
[ ] 하다　[ ] 벼루　[ ] 호두
[ ] 기러기　[ ] 미리
[ ] 그리기　[ ] 두부

Answer **1.** 1) ① 2) ② 3) ② 4) ② 5) ② **2.** 1) 아기 2) 그리기 3) 허리 4) 두부 5) 노루

Hangeul (3)

The tensed consonants are ‘doubled’ versions of the normal consonants, and the aspirated consonants have one extra horizontal line in each of them.
For pronunciation, the tensed version is pronounced without any release of air, but with ‘tightness’ in the throat, and the aspirated forms are pronounced with an extra-heavy explosive puff of air through the mouth.

Letter	ㄲ	ㅋ	ㄸ	ㅌ	ㅃ	ㅍ	ㅆ	ㅉ	ㅊ
Sound Value	[k']	[kʰ]	[t']	[tʰ]	[p']	[pʰ]	[s']	[tʃ']	[tʃʰ]
Writing Order	ㄲ	ㅋ	ㄸ	ㅌ	ㅃ	ㅍ	ㅆ	ㅉ	ㅊ

● Listen to the following. TRACK 04

가 까 카 　 다 따 타 　 바 빠 파 　 사 싸 　 자 짜 차

● Read the following words.

까치

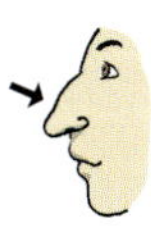
코

머리띠

타조

뿌리

포도

짜다

기차

쓰다

Write the following words.

까치	까치		
코	코		
머리띠	머리띠		
타조	타조		
뿌리	뿌리		
포도	포도		
짜다	짜다		
기차	기차		
쓰다	쓰다		

Exercise TRACK 04

1. Listen carefully, and choose the correct syllable.

1) ① 까 ② 따
2) ① 타 ② 파
3) ① 짜 ② 빠
4) ① 차 ② 카
5) ① 짜 ② 싸

2. Listen carefully, and number the words as you listen.

☐ 피다 ☐ 타이 ☐ 아빠
☐ 투수 [1)] 짜다 ☐ 뽀뽀 ☐ 까치

3. Listen carefully, and check(✓) the beginning sound of each word.

Example 1) 꼬마

	① [ㄱ]	② [ㄲ]	③ [ㅋ]
1)		✓	
2)			
3)			

	① [ㄷ]	② [ㄸ]	③ [ㅌ]
4)			
5)			
6)			

	① [ㅂ]	② [ㅃ]	③ [ㅍ]
7)			
8)			
9)			

	① [ㅅ]	② [ㅆ]
10)		
11)		

Answer **1.** 1)① 2)① 3)② 4)① 5)② **2.** 1) 짜다 2) 까치 3) 피다 4) 투수
5) 아빠 **3.** 1)② 2)③ 3)① 4)① 5)② 6)③ 7)③ 8)① 9)② 10)② 11)①

Hangeul (4)

Here are the vowels that are the combinations of the ten basic vowels.

Letter	ㅐ	ㅒ	ㅔ	ㅖ	ㅘ	ㅙ	ㅚ	ㅝ	ㅞ	ㅟ	ㅢ
Sound Value	[ɛ]	[yɛ]	[e]	[ye]	[wa]	[wɛ]	[ö/we]	[wə]	[we]	[ü/wi]	[ɨy]
Writing Order	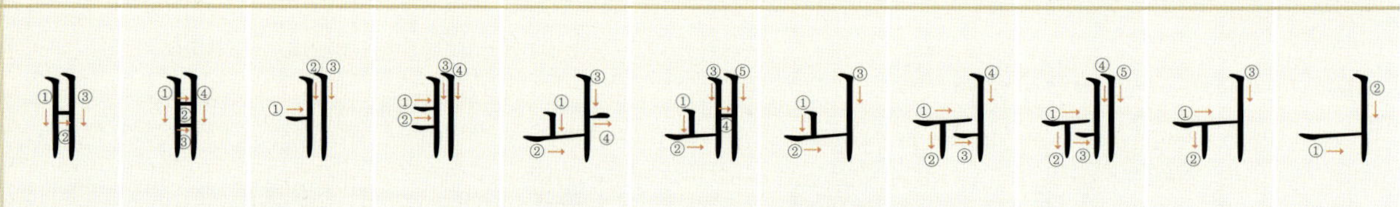										

Listen to the following. TRACK 05

애 얘 에 예 와 왜 외 워 웨 위 의

Read the following words.

 개미  얘기  가게  시계  과자

 돼지  회사  추워요  웨이터  귀  의사

Pronunciation Tips (1)

1. 'ㅔ' and 'ㅐ' are supposed to be distinguishable in pronunciation, but in many cases they are not distinguished these days.
2. 'ㅚ', 'ㅙ' and 'ㅞ' also tend to be pronounced the same as [wɛ] or [we].
3. 'ㅖ' is pronounced as [ㅖ] in '예' and '례', but in all other cases it can be pronounced as [ㅔ].
   예 → [예]　　실례 → [실례]
   시계 → [시계/시게]

Write the following words.

개미	개미		
얘기	얘기		
가게	가게		
시계	시계		
과자	과자		
돼지	돼지		
회사	회사		
추워요	추워요		
웨이터	웨이터		

귀	귀					

의사	의사		

● Exercise TRACK 05

1. Listen carefully, and choose the correct syllable.

1) ① 애 ② 예
2) ① 왜 ② 얘
3) ① 와 ② 외
4) ① 워 ② 웨
5) ① 위 ② 의

2. Listen carefully, and number the words as you listen.

	1) 개다	쇠고기	의자
위	예	왜	외우다

Answer **1.** 1) ① 2) ② 3) ① 4) ① 5) ②
2. 1) 개다 2) 위 3) 왜 4) 쇠고기 5) 의자

Hangeul (5)

A Hangeul syllable is made of a consonant and a vowel, and also can be made by adding one more consonant below the vowel. The added consonant is called 'batchim.' How to write a letter with a 'batchim' and without a 'batchim' are shown below.

가	그	떡	있

Korean consonants are pronounced in 7 representative sounds when they are located at the end of a syllable as a 'batchim.' For example, in syllables such as '박', '밬', '밖' which have 'ㄱ', 'ㅋ', 'ㄲ' as their 'batchims,' respectively all the 'batchims' will be pronounced as the representative sound 'ㄱ' and, therefore, the three syllables will be pronounced as the same sound [박]. And 'ㅇ', which has no sound value as the initial sound, is pronounced as [ŋ] as a 'batchim.' The respective batchims are pronounced as shown in the following table:

Batchim	Sound Value
ㄱ ㅋ ㄲ	[ㄱ]
ㄴ	[ㄴ]
ㄷ ㅅ ㅈ ㅊ ㅌ ㅎ ㅆ	[ㄷ]
ㄹ	[ㄹ]
ㅁ	[ㅁ]
ㅂ ㅍ	[ㅂ]
ㅇ	[ㅇ]

Listen to the following. TRACK 06

[ㄱ]	벽 wall 부엌 kitchen 밖 outside
[ㄴ]	눈 eye / snow
[ㄷ]	듣다 to hear / to listen 옷 clothes 낮 daytime 꽃 flower 밑 beneath 히읗 the character ㅎ 재미있다 interesting
[ㄹ]	팔 arm
[ㅁ]	곰 bear
[ㅂ]	집 house 잎 leaf
[ㅇ]	빵 bread

Pronunciation Tips ⟨2⟩

1. The final consonants that are compounds are pronounced with their representative sound only when it is positioned as the final syllable or when the first sound of the last syllable is a consonant.

   몫 [목] 흙 [흑]
   값 [갑] 읽다 [익따]
   앉다 [안따] 젊다 [점따]
   여덟 [여덜]

2. The final consonant of a syllable is pronounced as the initial sound of the following syllable when the latter begins with the consonant 'ㅇ'.

   저것은 [저거슨] 있어요 [이써요]
   젊어요 [절머요] 읽어요 [일거요]

● Read the following words.

[ㄱ]	벽 wall 부엌 kitchen 밖 outside 세탁기 washing machine 죽 porridge 미국 U.S.A. 수박 watermelon 우체국 post office 닭 chicken 흙 soil
[ㄴ]	눈 eye / snow 산 mountain 시간 time 돈 money 사진 photograph 신문 newspaper 도서관 library 진짜 real 부산 Busan 오렌지 orange 라면 ramen
[ㄷ]	걷다 to walk 옷 clothes 꽃 flower 밑 under / beneath 솥 pot 바깥 outside 빗 comb 낮 daytime
[ㄹ]	쌀 rice 발 foot 팔 arm 서울 Seoul 일본 Japan 교실 classroom 과일 fruit 불고기 bulgogi 할머니 grandmother 딸기 strawberry
[ㅁ]	봄 spring 엄마 mom 사람 person 김치 kimchi 인삼 ginseng 감기 cold 이름 name 점심 lunch 여름 summer 컴퓨터 computer
[ㅂ]	집 house 입 mouth 무릎 knee / lap 일곱 seven 앞 front 옆 side 지갑 wallet 숲 woods / forest
[ㅇ]	병원 hospital 창문 window 가방 bag 강 river 방 room 시장 market 사랑 love 청소 cleaning 영화 movie 화장실 rest room 동생 younger sibling

Write the following words.

수박	수박		
닭	닭		
시간	시간		
걷다	걷다		
낮	낮		
과일	과일		
이름	이름		
집	집		
옆	옆		
가방	가방		

Exercise

TRACK 06

1. Listen carefully, and choose the correct syllable.

1) ① 앞 ② 안
2) ① 갓 ② 감
3) ① 속 ② 솥
4) ① 징 ② 집
5) ① 돌 ② 돛

2. Listen carefully, and number the words as you listen.

☐ 공　☐ 문　[1)] 옷
☐ 죽　☐ 삽　☐ 꽃

3. Listen carefully, and check(✓) the final sound of each word.

Example 1) 산

	① [ㄱ]	② [ㄴ]	③ [ㄷ]	④ [ㄹ]	⑤ [ㅁ]	⑥ [ㅂ]	⑦ [ㅇ]
1)		✓					
2)							
3)							
4)							
5)							
6)							
7)							

Answer 1. 1) ② 2) ② 3) ① 4) ② 5) ① 2. 1) 옷 2) 공 3) 문 4) 삽 5) 죽 3. 1) ② 2) ⑦ 3) ③ 4) ① 5) ④ 6) ⑥ 7) ⑤

UNIT 2

Greetings & Introductions

인사와 소개

In This Unit

- Greetings 인사하기
- Introducing 소개하기
- Getting personal information 개인 정보 얻기

Expressions 표현

안녕하세요?	Hello. / How do you do?
안녕히 가세요.	Goodbye. (to a person who is leaving)
안녕히 계세요.	Goodbye. (to a person who is staying)
(만나서) 반가워요.	Nice to meet you.
이름이 뭐예요?	What's your name?

Vocabulary 어휘

Countries

미국 the United States of America
중국 China
일본 Japan
인도 India
호주 Australia
영국 the United Kingdom
독일 Germany
프랑스 France
캐나다 Canada
한국 Korea
러시아 Russia

Occupations

선생님 teacher
학생 student
의사 doctor
요리사 chef
은행원 bank clerk
기자 reporter
회사원 company employee
연구원 researcher

Others

여기 here
씨 Mr., Miss, Mrs., Ms.
저 I
이분 this person
사람 person
이름 name
국적 nationality
직업 job / occupation
주소 address
전화 telephone

Key Dialogues 핵심 대화

Greetings

TRACK 07

Notes

"안녕하세요?" is the most common greeting used when meeting someone. It can be used to either greet someone you meet for the first time or greet someone you see every day.

A 안녕하세요?

B 안녕하세요?

A Hello.

B Hello.

Notes

"안녕히 가세요." is "Goodbye," used to a person who is leaving and "안녕히 계세요." is "Goodbye," used to a person who is staying.

A 안녕히 가세요.

B 안녕히 계세요.

A Good bye.

B Good bye.

Introducing yourself

TRACK 07

A 안녕하세요?
저는 김재민이에요.

B 안녕하세요, 재민 씨?
저는 애니예요.

A How do you do?
I'm Jaemin Kim.

B How do you do, Jaemin?
I'm Annie.

Grammar Points

N은/는

'은/는' follows a noun, indicating that it is the topic under discussion.

nouns ending with a vowel + 는 : 저 → 저는

nouns ending with a consonant + 은 : 이분 → 이분은

▶ Grammar Reference p.142

Grammar Points

N-이에요/예요

'-이에요/예요' are sentence endings expressing identification and are attached to nouns.

nouns ending with a vowel + -예요 : 애니 → 애니예요

nouns ending with a consonant + -이에요 : 학생 → 학생이에요

▶ Grammar Reference p.142

Practice

1 Circle the correct particle.

1) 저(은 / 는) 애니예요.
2) 마이클(은 / 는) 미국 사람이에요.
3) 여기(은 / 는) 토니 씨예요.
4) 이분(은 / 는) 선생님이에요.

2 Fill in the blanks by choosing the correct form between '-이에요/예요'.

1) 저는 학생__________.
2) 웨이 씨는 중국 사람__________.
3) 저는 쿠마르__________.
4) 다니엘은 의사__________.

Answer 1 1) 는 2) 은 3) 는 4) 은 2 1) 이에요 2) 이에요 3) 예요 4) 예요

Notes

'씨' is a term of address that can be added at the end of someone's name. It can be used with either the first name or full name, regardless of gender. It is rather impolite to use '씨' with the last name only.

재민 씨 (O) 김재민 씨 (O)
김 씨 (X)

Introducing another person

TRACK 07

A 여기는 크리스 씨예요.

여기는 김재민 씨예요.

B 안녕하세요? 김재민이에요.

C 안녕하세요? 크리스예요.

만나서 반가워요.

A This is Chris.

This is Jaemin Kim.

B How do you do?

I'm Jaemin Kim.

C How do you do? I'm Chris.

Nice to meet you.

Notes

The speaker can use '여기', referring to those who are younger than or at the same level as himself, but when referring to those who are older or higher in position than himself, he must use '이분'.

Notes

When it is obvious to the other person what the topic is, the topic is generally omitted.

(저는) 애니예요.

However, when it is necessary to make the topic clear, the topic is not omitted.

Getting personal information

TRACK 07

Grammar Points

네, 아니요

For questions using 'N-이에요/예요?' patterns, you answer using '네' or '아니요'.

▶ Grammar Reference p.142

A 로버트 씨는 의사예요?

B 네, 의사예요.

A Are you a doctor, Robert?

B Yes, I am a doctor.

A 웨이 씨는 일본 사람이에요?

B 아니요, 중국 사람이에요.

A Are you Japanese, Wei?

B No, I'm Chinese.

Practice

● With your partner, ask and answer using the pictures below.

1) 

양양
(중국 사람, 학생)

2) 

키샨
(인도 사람, 요리사)

3) 

마이클
(미국 사람, 은행원)

4) 

크리스
(호주 사람, 선생님)

Conversation Drills 대화 연습

Conversation 1 TRACK 08

A How do you do?
B How do you do? I'm Chris.
A Chris, are you American?
B No, I'm Australian.
A Chris, are you a teacher?
B Yes, I'm a teacher.

A 안녕하세요?

B 안녕하세요? 저는 크리스예요.

A 크리스 씨는 미국 사람이에요?

B 아니요, 저는 호주 사람이에요.

A 크리스 씨는 선생님이에요?

B 네, 저는 선생님이에요.

Check it

1. 크리스 씨는 미국 사람이에요.
   T F

2. 크리스 씨는 선생님이에요.
   T F

Answer 1. F 2. T

Practice the dialogue with your partner.

1)	2)	3)	4)
크리스	마르틴	웨이	안나
크리스 / 미국 사람	마르틴 / 영국 사람	웨이 / 일본 사람	안나 / 독일 사람
호주 사람	독일 사람	중국 사람	프랑스 사람
크리스 / 선생님	마르틴 / 기자	웨이 / 은행원	안나 / 요리사
선생님	기자	은행원	요리사

Conversation 2

TRACK 08

A Jaemin, this is Chris.

Chris, this is Jaemin.

B How do you do?

C How do you do? Nice to meet you.

A 재민 씨, 여기는 크리스 씨예요.

크리스 씨, 여기는 재민 씨예요.

B 안녕하세요?

C 안녕하세요? 만나서 반가워요.

Check it

1. Chris and Jaemin meet for the first time.

   T F

2. Jaemin is introducing Chris.

   T F

Answer 1. T 2. F

Practice the dialogue with your partner.

1) 재민 / 크리스

2) 웨이 / 마이클

3) 애니 / 미사코

4) 마르틴 / 수미

Tasks & Activities 과제

1. Pair work

Look at the ID cards below, then ask questions about them to your partner.

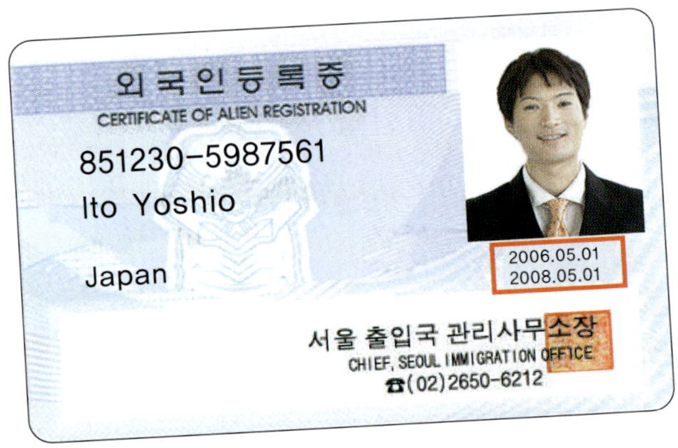

이름이 뭐예요?

첸웨이예요.

한국 사람이에요?

아니요, 중국 사람이에요.

2. Group work

Ask the following questions to each other while exchanging business cards.

1. 이름이 뭐예요?			
2. 한국 사람이에요?			
3. 선생님이에요?			

이름	이름	이름
국적	국적	국적
직업	직업	직업

Listening 듣기

TRACK 09

1. Listen carefully, and choose the correct picture.

1)

① 선생님

② 학생

③ 회사원

2)

① 캐나다

② 한국

③ 러시아

2. Listen carefully, and choose the picture that best fits the dialogue.

①

②

③

3. Listen carefully, and match the person with the correct nationality.

1) 제니

2) 앤디

① 

캐나다

② 

미국

③ 

영국

4. Listen carefully, and match the person with the correct occupation.

1) 제니

2) 앤디

① 

② 

③ 

Answer **1.** 1) ③ 2) ③ **2.** ②
3. 1) ② 2) ① **4.** 1) ① 2) ③

Reading & Writing 읽기와 쓰기

Read the following and write a paragraph introducing yourself.

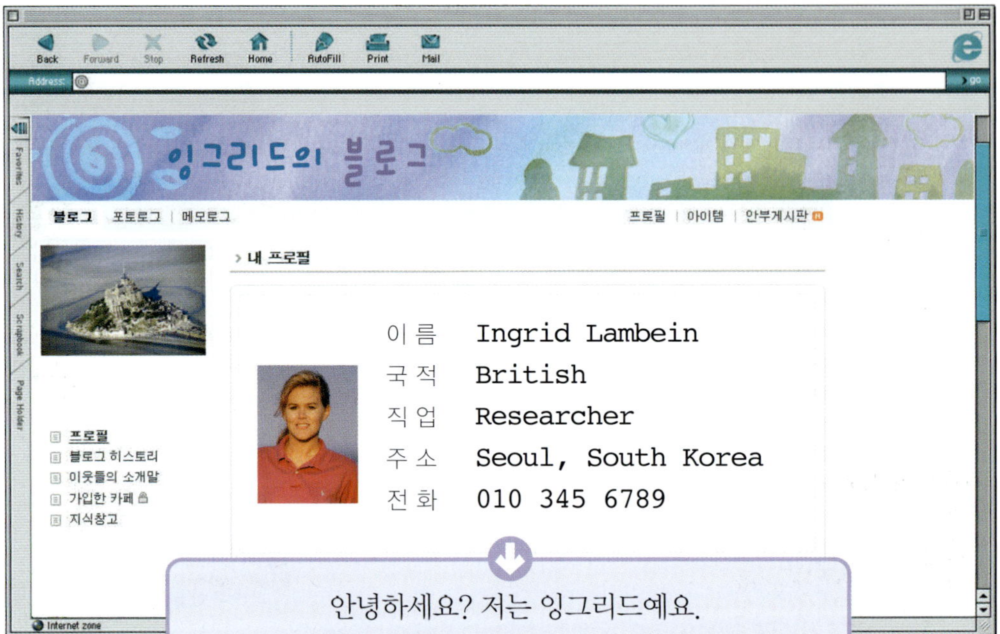

안녕하세요? 저는 잉그리드예요.
저는 영국 사람이에요.
저는 연구원이에요.
만나서 반가워요.

Now I can...

- ☐ greet
- ☐ introduce myself
- ☐ introduce another person
- ☐ get personal information

in Korean.

Additional Expressions 추가 표현

Occupations

사업가 businessman

소방관 fire fighter

경찰 police

배우 actor / actress

우체부 mail carrier

미용사 hairdresser

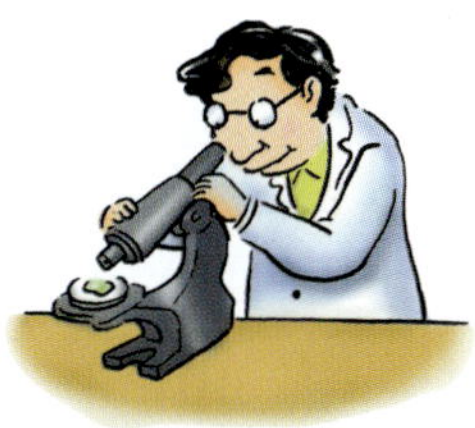
과학자 scientist

기술자 technician

교수 professor

변호사 lawyer

모델 model

회계사 accountant

UNIT 3

Restaurant

식당

In This Unit

- Ordering food 주문하기
- Making requests (1) 요청하기 (1)

Expressions 표현

어서 오세요.	Welcome.
뭐 드릴까요?	What would you like to have?
여기요.	Excuse me.
잠깐만 기다리세요.	Just a moment, please.
여기 있어요.	Here it is.

Vocabulary 어휘

Verbs

주다 to give
읽다 to read
가다 to go
오다 to come
앉다 to sit down
기다리다 to wait
쉬다 to rest
쓰다 to write

Food

불고기 bulgogi
냉면 naengmyeon
비빔밥 bibimbap
라면 ramen
김밥 gimbap
사과 apple
오렌지 orange
김치 kimchi
햄버거 hamburger
빵 bread

Drinks

우유 milk
콜라 cola
맥주 beer
물 water
커피 coffee
주스 juice
홍차 black tea
녹차 green tea

Numbers

하나 one
둘 two
셋 three
넷 four
다섯 five
여섯 six
일곱 seven
여덟 eight
아홉 nine
열 ten
한 one
두 two
세 three
네 four

Counting Units

병 (for bottles)
개 (for general items)
잔 (for glasses or cups)

Others

메뉴 menu
좀 please
더 more
몇 how many

Key Dialogues 핵심 대화

Ordering at a restaurant (1)

TRACK 10

A 어서 오세요. 뭐 드릴까요?

B 불고기 주세요.

A Welcome. What would you like to have?

B I'd like to have bulgogi.

Grammar Points

V-(으)세요

'-(으)세요' is used to make requests, suggestions, or commands politely.

verb stems ending with a vowel + -세요 : 주다 → 주세요

verb stems ending with a consonant + -으세요 : 읽다 → 읽으세요

▶ Grammar Reference p.142

Notes

"뭐 드릴까요?" is an expression used when asking what a customer wants.

Grammar Points

N 주세요

Adding '주세요' after N means requesting N for the speaker.

▶ Grammar Reference p.142

Practice

1 Change the words below as shown in the example.

가다 → 가세요

1) 오다 →
2) 읽다 →
3) 앉다 →
4) 기다리다 →

2 You are at a restaurant. Order the following food.

1)  냉면 ________.

2)  비빔밥 ________.

3)  라면 ________.

4)  김밥 ________.

Answer **1** 1) 오세요 2) 읽으세요 3) 앉으세요 4) 기다리세요 **2** 1) 냉면 주세요 2) 비빔밥 주세요 3) 라면 주세요 4) 김밥 주세요

Ordering at a restaurant (2)

TRACK 10

A 뭐 드릴까요?

B 냉면 둘 주세요.

A What would you like to have?

B Please give me two bowls of naengmyeon.

Grammar Points

하나, 둘, 셋, 넷,…

'하나, 둘, 셋, 넷,…' is the Korean numbering system. This is used for counting people or things in Korean.

1 – 하나	6 – 여섯
2 – 둘	7 – 일곱
3 – 셋	8 – 여덟
4 – 넷	9 – 아홉
5 – 다섯	10 – 열

▶ Grammar Reference p.142

Practice

1 Fill in the blanks.

1	2	3	4	5	6	7	8	9	10
하나			넷	다섯		일곱			열

2 Make an order after reading the menu.

메뉴
냉면
불고기
라면
김밥

Answer 1 둘, 셋, 여섯, 여덟, 아홉

Ordering at a restaurant (3)

TRACK 10

Grammar Points

병, 개, 잔

'병' is a counting unit. In Korean, there is a variety of counting units to count objects. '개' is used widely to count general inanimate items, '병' for bottles and '잔' for cups or glasses.

▶ Grammar Reference p.143

A 뭐 드릴까요?

B 콜라 한 병하고 맥주 두 병 주세요.

A What would you like to have?

B Please give me a bottle of cola and two bottles of beer.

Grammar Points

N하고 N'

'하고' is used to connect two nouns with the meaning 'and.'

▶ Grammar Reference p.143

Practice

1 Write down the following using '하고'.

1)  사과 +  오렌지　　2)  우유 +  콜라

______________________　　______________________

2 Match each item with the appropriate counting unit.

개　　병　　잔

Answer **1** 1) 사과하고 오렌지 2) 우유하고 콜라 **2** 개 – 병 – 잔 –

Asking for more

TRACK 10

A 여기요. 김치 좀 더 주세요.

B 잠깐만 기다리세요.

A Excuse me. Please give me some more kimchi.

B Just a moment, please.

Notes

"여기요." literally means "Here," but at a restaurant it is used to get the waiter/waitress's attention.

Notes

'좀' makes the expression sound softer and more polite.

물 좀 주세요.

Notes

When asking for more, add '더' in front of '주세요'.

물 좀 더 주세요.

Conversation Drills 대화 연습

Conversation

TRACK 11

A Welcome. What shall I get you?

B Give me some bulgogi and two bottles of beer, please.

A OK. Just a moment, please.

...

B Excuse me. Give me some more kimchi, please.

A Here it is.

A 어서 오세요. 뭐 드릴까요?

B 불고기하고 맥주 두 병 주세요.

A 네, 잠깐만 기다리세요.

• • •

B 여기요. 김치 좀 더 주세요.

A 네, 여기 있어요.

Check it

What did the customer order?

① 

② 

Answer ②

Look at the menu and make an order together with your partner.

Tasks & Activities 과제

Group work

Roll a die and order the items in the box in Korean. On "쉬세요," you have to skip a turn and let your partner roll the die. If you fail to do the required task such as counting numbers from one to ten in Korean, then you have to let your partner roll the die again.

Example

커피 1 → 커피 한 잔 주세요.

Listening 듣기

TRACK 12

1. **Listen carefully, and write down the number of things that were ordered.**

1) 햄버거 ________ 개

2) 오렌지 주스 ________ 잔

3) 커피 ________ 잔

4) 맥주 ________ 병

2. **Listen carefully, and choose the correct picture that shows the items that were ordered.**

1)

①

②

③

2)

①

②

③

3)

①

②

③

3. Listen to the sentences, and match each sentence with the correct picture.

1) ●

2) ●

3) ●

4) ●

① 

② 

③ 

④ 

⑤ 

Answer **1.** 1) 2 2) 3 3) 1 4) 5
2. 1) ③ 2) ② 3) ① **3.** 1) ④
2) ② 3) ① 4) ③

Reading & Writing 읽기와 쓰기

Read the following carefully, and write down what the customers ordered on the order sheet.

주 문 서

메 뉴	수량
비빔밥	1

Now I can...

- ☐ order food at a restaurant
- ☐ make a request
- ☐ count numbers

in Korean.

Answer 비빔밥1, 김밥3, 콜라2

Additional Expressions 추가 표현

Food and tableware

컵 cup / glass

접시 plate

밥 rice

반찬 side dishes

생선 fish

돼지고기 pork

쇠고기 beef

닭고기 chicken

된장찌개
beanpaste stew

국
broth / soup

간장
soy sauce

고추장
red pepper paste

소금 salt

한식 Korean food

일식 Japanese food

양식 western food

UNIT 4

Shopping

쇼핑

In This Unit

- Describing things with demonstratives 지시어로 표현하기
- Asking prices 물건 값 묻고 말하기
- Buying things 물건 사기

Expressions 표현

이거는 뭐예요?	What's this?
얼마예요?	How much (is it)?
너무 비싸요.	It's too expensive.
좀 깎아 주세요.	Please give me a discount.
하나에 얼마예요?	How much is it for one?
모두 얼마예요?	How much is it altogether?

Vocabulary 어휘

Demonstratives

이거 this (one)
그거 that (one)
저거 that (one)
저 that
이 this
그 that

Nouns

시계 watch / clock
우산 umbrella
볼펜 ball-point pen
휴대 전화 cellular phone / mobile
담배 cigarette
한국어 Korean (language)
사전 dictionary
신문 newspaper
가방 bag
카메라 camera
치마 skirt
연필 pencil
책 book
모자 hat / cap
구두 dress shoes
바지 trousers / pants
공책 notebook
돈 money

Numbers

일 one
이 two
삼 three
사 four
오 five
육 six
칠 seven
팔 eight
구 nine
십 ten
백 hundred
천 thousand
만 ten thousand
십만 hundred thousand

Others

있다 to have
없다 not to have
뭐 what
얼마 how much
원 KRW / won (Korean money)
그럼 then / in that case
제 my

Key Dialogues 핵심 대화

Asking if someone has an item

TRACK 13

A 시계가 있어요?

B 네, 있어요.

A Do you have a watch?

B Yes, I do.

A 우산이 있어요?

B 아니요, 없어요.

A Do you have an umbrella?

B No, I don't.

Grammar Points

N이/가 있어요/없어요

'N이/가 있어요' means the subject has N, and 'N이/가 없어요' means the subject doesn't have N.

nouns ending with a vowel + 가 : 시계 → 시계가

nouns ending with a consonant + 이 : 우산 → 우산이

Raising the intonation at the end without any changes in word order makes the sentence a question.

우산이 있어요. ↘

우산이 있어요? ↗

▶ Grammar Reference p.144

Practice

Pair up, and ask each other whether he / she has the following items or not.

볼펜이 있어요?

볼펜

네, 있어요.

아니요, 없어요.

휴대 전화

담배

한국어 사전

신문

우산

Asking the name of things with demonstratives

TRACK 13

A 이거는 뭐예요?

B 그거는 사전이에요.

A What's this?

B That is a dictionary.

A 저거는 뭐예요?

B 저거는 가방이에요.

A What's that?

B That is a bag.

Grammar Points

이거, 그거, 저거

'이거, 그거, 저거' are used to point at things.
'이거' is used to point at the thing close to the speaker.
'그거' is used to point at the thing close to the listener.
'저거' is used to point at the thing away from both the speaker and the listener.

▶ Grammar Reference p.144

Practice

● Ask your partner the name of each object using '이거, 그거, 저거'.

Describing things with demonstratives

TRACK 13

A 저 책은 한국어 책이에요?

B 네, 한국어 책이에요.

A Is that a Korean book?

B Yes, it is.

Grammar Points

이 N, 그 N, 저 N

'이, 그, 저' are always followed by a noun and used to point at things or people.
'이 N' indicates a thing or person close to the speaker.
'그 N' indicates a thing or person close to the listener.
'저 N' indicates a thing or person away from both the speaker and the listener.

▶ Grammar Reference p.144

Practice

Complete the following sentences using '이 N, 그 N, 저 N'.

1) 이 시계 주세요.

2) ________ 주세요.

3) ________ 주세요.

4) ________ 주세요.

5) ________ 주세요.

6) ________ 주세요.

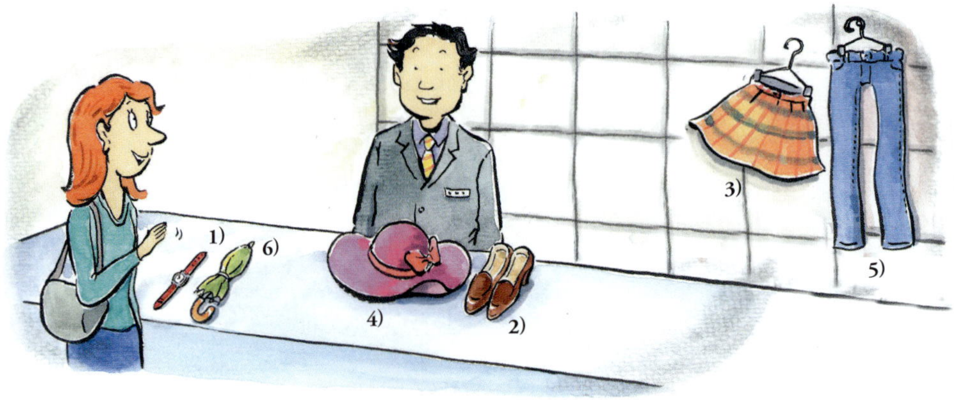

Answer 1) 이 시계 2) 그 구두 3) 저 치마 4) 그 모자 5) 저 바지 6) 이 우산

Asking prices

TRACK 13

A 이 사과는 얼마예요?

B 오백 원이에요.

A How much is this apple?

B It's 500 won.

A 이 사과는 하나에 얼마예요?

B 이천 원이에요.

A 너무 비싸요. 좀 깎아 주세요.

A How much is one of these apples?

B It's 2,000 won.

A It's too expensive. Please give me a discount.

Grammar Points

일, 이, 삼, 사,⋯

For money, the following numbering system is used

1	일
10	십
100	백
1,000	천
10,000	만
100,000	십만

For prices, '원' (the Korean monetary unit) is used.

▶ Grammar Reference p.144

Notes

When asking the price of one item, you say "하나에 얼마예요?"

Notes

When you bargain over the prices at the market, you can say "너무 비싸요. 좀 깎아 주세요."

Practice

Ask your partner the price of the following products.

이 신문은 얼마예요?

신문 500원

오백 원이에요.

우산 8,500원

가방 35,000원

치마 29,900원

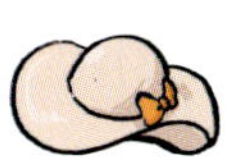

모자 7,300원

카메라 116,000원

바지 48,000원

Conversation Drills 대화 연습

Conversation

TRACK 14

A Welcome.
B Do you have a ball-point pen?
A Yes, we do.
B How much is it for one?
A It's 1,000 won.
B Give me two, please.
A Here you are.
B How much is that notebook?
A It's 2,000 won.
B Then give me one of that, please.
How much is it altogether?
A It's 4,000 won.

A 어서 오세요.
B 볼펜 있어요?
A 네, 있어요.
B 하나에 얼마예요?
A 1,000원이에요.
B 두 개 주세요.
A 여기 있어요.
B 저 공책은 얼마예요?
A 2,000원이에요.
B 그럼 저 공책 하나 주세요.
모두 얼마예요?
A 4,000원이에요.

Check it

1. 볼펜이 있어요?
   ① 네, 있어요.
   ② 아니요, 없어요.
2. 공책은 하나에 얼마예요?
   ① 1,000원 ② 2,000원

Answer 1. ① 2. ②

Practice the dialogue with your partner.

	1)	2)	3)	4)
	볼펜 1,000원	신문 500원	우유 600원	사과 2,000원
	공책 2,000원	담배 2,500원	맥주 2,000원	오렌지 1,000원

Tasks & Activities 과제

Class Activity

Divide the class into two groups. Then the members of one group play the shop owners and the members of the other group play the customers. The customers ask the price and buy things going around the classroom.

Listening 듣기

TRACK 15

1. **Listen carefully, and mark O if the clerk has the item in question, and mark X if he doesn't.**

1) 
( )

2) 
( )

3) 
( )

2. **Listen carefully, and choose the correct price.**

1) 
(30,000원 40,000원)

2) 
(1,000원 2,000원)

3) 
(20,000원 50,000원)

3. **Listen to the dialogue, and choose the correct items purchased.**

1) ① 
20,000원

② 
30,000원

③ 
20,000원

2) ① 
500원

② 
1,500원

③ 
2,500원

3) ① 
2,000원

② 
3,000원

③ 
3,000원

Answer 1. 1) O 2) X 3) O 2. 1) 30,000원 2) 2,000원 3) 50,000원 3. 1) ① 2) ③ 3) ③

Reading & Writing 읽기와 쓰기

1. **Read the following dialogues, and connect each dialogue with the correct picture.**

1) A 사과 한 개에 얼마예요?
B 천 원이에요.
A 다섯 개 주세요.
B 여기 있어요.

① 

2) A 어서 오세요.
B 한국어 사전 있어요?
A 네. 여기 있어요.
B 얼마예요?

② 

3) A 이 바지 얼마예요?
B 이만 오천 원이에요.
A 너무 비싸요. 좀 깎아 주세요.
B 이만 삼천 원 주세요.

③ 

Answer 1. 1) ② 2) ③ 3) ①

2. Complete the following dialogues using sentences provided in the box.

좀 깎아 주세요.	얼마예요?	한 병에 얼마예요?
영어 사전 있어요?	세 병 주세요.	이 모자 얼마예요?

1)

A 맥주 한 병에 얼마예요?

B 이천 원이에요.

A ______________________

B 여기 있어요.

2)

A 어서 오세요.

B ______________________

A 네, 여기 있어요.

B ______________________

3)

A ______________________

B 이만 원이에요.

A 너무 비싸요. ______________________

B 만 팔천 원 주세요.

Now I can...

- ☐ describe things using demonstratives
- ☐ ask prices
- ☐ buy items at a store

in Korean.

Answer 2. 1) 세 병 주세요. 2) 영어 사전 있어요? 얼마예요? 3) 이 모자 얼마예요? 좀 깎아 주세요.

Additional Expressions 추가 표현

Counting units for various items

개 한 개, 두 개, 세 개, 네 개, …

병 한 병, 두 병, 세 병, 네 병, …

잔 한 잔, 두 잔, 세 잔, 네 잔, …

장 한 장, 두 장, 세 장, 네 장, …

권 한 권, 두 권, 세 권, 네 권, …

송이 한 송이, 두 송이, 세 송이, 네 송이, …

마리 한 마리, 두 마리, 세 마리, 네 마리, …

벌 한 벌, 두 벌, 세 벌, 네 벌, …

켤레 한 켤레, 두 켤레, 세 켤레, 네 켤레, …

대 한 대, 두 대, 세 대, 네 대, …

UNIT 5

Daily Life
일상생활

In This Unit

- Talking about daily life 일상생활 말하기
- Expressing 'come and go' 이동 표현하기
- Linking two sentences 이어서 말하기

Expressions 표현

지금 뭐 해요? What are you doing now?

어디에 가요? Where are you going?

Vocabulary 어휘

Places

공원 park | 식당 restaurant | 학교 school | 병원 hospital
산 mountain | 시장 market | 집 house

Time

지금 now | 오늘 today | 내일 tomorrow | 요즘 these days / nowadays

Food

밥 steamed rice | 피자 pizza | 포도 grape(s) | 바나나 banana
고기 meat | 스파게티 spaghetti

Verbs

하다 to do | 사다 to buy | 운동하다 to exercise / to work out | 청소하다 to clean
먹다 to eat | 배우다 to learn | 빨래하다 to do laundry
만나다 to meet | 입다 to wear / to put on | 공부하다 to study | 가르치다 to teach
좋아하다 to like | 마시다 to drink | 보다 to see / to watch

Nouns

친구 friend | 날씨 weather | 텔레비전 television | 공부 study / learning
옷 clothes | 길 road / way | 영화 movie | 질문 question
영어 English (language) | 운동 exercise / workout | 태권도 taekwondo

Adjectives

맛있다 tasty / delicious | 싸다 cheap | 복잡하다 crowded / jammed | 재미있다 interesting
따뜻하다 warm | 좋다 good

Interrogatives

어디 where | 뭘 what

Others

안 not | 그리고 and | 아주 very | 우리 we / our

Words that go together

날씨가 좋다 The weather is fine.

길이 복잡하다 The road is crowded.

날씨가 따뜻하다 The weather is warm.

Key Dialogues 핵심 대화

Talking about daily life

TRACK 16

A 지금 뭐 해요?

B 밥을 먹어요.

A What are you doing now?

B I'm eating my meal.

A 오늘 뭐 해요?

B 친구를 만나요.

A What are you doing today?

B I'm seeing a friend.

Grammar Points

A/V-아요/어요

'-아요/어요' are casual sentence endings and make present tense verbs and adjectives.

verb or adjective stem's last vowels ending with 'ㅏ' or 'ㅗ' + -아요:
만나다 → 만나요

verbs or adjectives ending with '하다', 하다 → 해요 :
좋아하다 → 좋아해요

In all other cases, add '-어요' :
먹다 → 먹어요

▶ Grammar Reference p.145

Grammar Points

N을/를

'을/를' are attached to the end of a noun to make it the direct object of the verb.

nouns ending with a vowel + 를 :
친구 → 친구를

nouns ending with a consonant + 을 : 밥 → 밥을

▶ Grammar Reference p.145

Practice

1 Change the following into the '-아요/어요' form.

1) 사다 → ________
2) 배우다 → ________
3) 맛있다 → ________
4) 따뜻하다 → ________

2 Circle the correct particle.

1) 마이클 씨는 옷(을 / 를) 입어요.
2) 애니 씨는 영어(을 / 를) 배워요.
3) 재민 씨는 친구(을 / 를) 만나요.
4) 미사코 씨는 비빔밥(을 / 를) 좋아해요.

Answer **1** 1) 사요 2) 배워요 3) 맛있어요 4) 따뜻해요 **2** 1) 을 2) 를 3) 를 4) 을

Expressing movement

TRACK 16

Grammar Points

N에 가다/오다

'가다' is used when one is going away from the place where the dialogue is taking place. '오다' is used when one is coming toward the place where the dialogue is taking place.
To show the destination, '에' is added after the place.

▶ Grammar Reference p.146

A 어디에 가요?

B 공원에 가요.

A Where are you going?

B I'm going to a park.

Practice

With your partner, talk about where you're going using the places provided below.

어디에 가요?

산

산에 가요.

식당

시장

학교

집

Expressing negation

TRACK 16

Grammar Points

안 A/V

The negating adverb '안' comes before a verb or an adjective and marks negation.

▶▶ Grammar Reference p.146

A 고기를 먹어요?

B 아니요, 안 먹어요.

A Do you eat meat?

B No, I don't.

Practice

Answer the question using '안'.

1) **A** 커피를 마셔요?
   B 아니요, ________________.

2) **A** 내일 친구를 만나요?
   B 아니요, ________________.

3) **A** 오늘 학교에 가요?
   B 아니요, ________________.

4) **A** 요즘 운동해요?
   B 아니요, ________________.

Answer 1) 안 마셔요 2) 안 만나요 3) 안 가요 4) 운동 안 해요

Describing a person or a thing

TRACK 16

A 김치가 맛있어요?

B 네, 맛있어요.

A Is the kimchi delicious?

B Yes, it is delicious.

A 가방이 싸요?

B 네, 싸요.

A Is the bag cheap?

B Yes, it is cheap.

Grammar Points

N이/가 A

The subject marker '-이/가' is attached to a noun to indicate that it is the subject of the sentence.

nouns ending with a vowel + 가 : 김치 → 김치가

nouns ending with a consonant + 이 : 가방 → 가방이

▶ Grammar Reference p.146

Practice

Fill in the blanks with the correct particle between '이' and '가'.

1) 옷(　　　) 싸요.
2) 날씨(　　　) 좋아요.
3) 길(　　　) 복잡해요.
4) 한국어(　　　) 재미있어요.

Answer 1) 이 2) 가 3) 이 4) 가

Linking two sentences

TRACK 16

Grammar Points

그리고

'그리고' is used to link two sentences on an equal basis.

▶ Grammar Reference p.146

A 오늘 뭐 해요?

B 한국어를 공부해요.

그리고 친구를 만나요.

A What are you doing today?

B I'm studying Korean.

And I'm meeting a friend.

Practice

Look at the pictures below, and complete the sentences.

 옷을 사다 +  집에 가다

1) 미사코 씨는 ______________________.

______________________.

 한국어를 배우다 +  친구를 만나다

2) 크리스 씨는 ______________________.

______________________.

 밥을 먹다 +  녹차를 마시다

3) 애니 씨는 ______________________.

______________________.

 텔레비전을 보다 +  운동을 하다

4) 쿠마르 씨는 ______________________.

______________________.

Answer 1) 옷을 사요, 그리고 집에 가요 2) 한국어를 배워요, 그리고 친구를 만나요 3) 밥을 먹어요, 그리고 녹차를 마셔요 4) 텔레비전을 봐요, 그리고 운동을 해요

Conversation Drills 대화 연습

Conversation 1

TRACK 17

A Lydia, are you going to school today?

B No, I'm not.

A Then what are you doing?

B Exercising. And watching a movie.

A 리디아 씨, 오늘 학교에 가요?

B 아니요, 안 가요.

A 그럼 뭐 해요?

B 운동해요. 그리고 영화를 봐요.

Check it

What is Lydia doing today?
Check all that applies.

① 학교에 가요.
② 운동해요.
③ 영화를 봐요.

Answer ②, ③

Practice the dialogue with your partner.

1) 학교	2) 산	3) 병원
운동하다 / 영화를 보다	청소하다 / 빨래하다	한국어를 배우다 / 친구를 만나다

Conversation 2

TRACK 17

A Miho, do you like juice?

B No, I don't.

A Do you like coffee?

B Yes, coffee is tasty.

A 미호 씨, 주스를 좋아해요?

B 아니요, 안 좋아해요.

A 커피를 좋아해요?

B 네, 좋아해요. 커피가 맛있어요.

Check it

미호 씨는 커피를 좋아해요.

T F

Answer T

Practice the dialogue with your partner.

 커피  녹차  콜라  주스  우유

 비빔밥  불고기  피자  스파게티

 사과  포도  오렌지  바나나

Tasks & Activities 과제

Group work

Ask your classmates the following questions, and write down the answers in the blanks.

이 름 / 질 문			
커피를 좋아해요?			
녹차를 마셔요?			
불고기를 먹어요?			
오늘 친구를 만나요?			
김치가 맛있어요?			
날씨가 따뜻해요?			
한국어가 재미있어요?			

Listening 듣기

TRACK 18

1. Listen carefully, and choose all the activities Jaemin is doing today.

①

②

③

④

2. Listen carefully, and mark O if Annie likes the food, and mark X if she doesn't.

① 불고기

② 비빔밥

③ 김밥

④ 냉면

3. Connect the name of each person with the correct picture.

1) 리디아 ●

2) 애니 ●

3) 레이 ●

4) 미사코 ●

① 

② 

③ 

④ 

⑤ 

Answer 1. ③, ④ 2. ① O ② O ③ X ④ O 3. 1) ① 2) ③ 3) ② 4) ⑤

Reading & Writing 읽기와 쓰기

1. Read the following, and check(✓) "T" for true and "F" for false.

크리스 씨는 운동을 아주 좋아해요. 태권도를 해요. 미사코 씨는 운동을 안 좋아해요. 미사코 씨는 영화를 좋아해요. 오늘 영화를 봐요. 쿠마르 씨는 공부를 좋아해요. 쿠마르 씨는 오늘 한국어를 배워요. 그리고 책을 읽어요.

1) 크리스 씨는 태권도를 해요. T F
2) 미사코 씨는 운동을 좋아해요. T F
3) 쿠마르 씨는 책을 안 읽어요. T F

2. Referring to the example above, write about your friends.

Now I can...

- ☐ talk about my daily routines
- ☐ express movement
- ☐ express negation
- ☐ describe a person or a thing
- ☐ link two sentences

in Korean.

Answer 1. 1) T 2) F 3) F

Additional Expressions 추가 표현

Daily life expressions

일어나다 to get up

세수하다 to wash one's face

이를 닦다 to brush one's teeth

버스를 타다 to take a bus

일을 하다 to work

전화(를) 하다
to make a phone call

요리(를) 하다 / 음식을 만들다
to cook

설거지(를) 하다
to wash the dishes

샤워(를) 하다 to take a shower

자다 to sleep

UNIT 6

Time
시간

In This Unit

- Talking about time 시간 말하기
- Talking about days of the week 요일 말하기
- Expressing contrast 대조 표현하기

Expressions 표현

지금 몇 시예요?	What time is it now?
오늘 무슨 요일이에요?	What day is it today?
오늘 뭐 해요?	What are you doing today?

Vocabulary 어휘

Time

시 o'clock
분 minute(s)
주말 weekend
오전 morning / a.m.
오후 afternoon / p.m.
반 half

Days of the week

요일 a day of the week
월요일 Monday
화요일 Tuesday
수요일 Wednesday
목요일 Thursday
금요일 Friday
토요일 Saturday
일요일 Sunday

Interrogatives

무슨 what kind of
언제 when

Others

일어나다 to get up
쯤 about / around
자다 to sleep
나 I
백화점 department store
비싸다 expensive
일하다 to work
샤워하다 to take a shower

Key Dialogues 핵심 대화

Telling time

TRACK 19

Grammar Points

_ 시 _ 분

When telling time, use the number system of '한, 두, 세, 네,…' for the hours, and use '일, 이, 삼, 사,…' for the minutes.

▶ Grammar Reference p.146

A 지금 몇 시예요?

B 한 시 이십 분이에요.

A What time is it now?

B It's one twenty.

Practice

Look at the pictures below, and fill in the blanks in Korean.

1)  ________ 시 ________ 분

2)  ________ 시 ________ 분

3)  ________ 시 ________ 분

4)  ________ 시 ________ 분

Answer 1) 세, 십 2) 다섯, 이십오 3) 여덟, 삼십 4) 열두, 사십오

Expressing days of the week

TRACK 19

A 오늘 무슨 요일이에요?

B 화요일이에요.

A What day is it today?

B It's Tuesday.

Grammar Points

요일

Days of the week in Korean

월요일 – Monday
화요일 – Tuesday
수요일 – Wednesday
목요일 – Thursday
금요일 – Friday
토요일 – Saturday
일요일 – Sunday

▶ Grammar Reference p.147

Notes

When asking about days of the week, add '요일' after '무슨' to make the sentence, "무슨 요일이에요?"

Practice

Write the correct days in the blanks.

Monday	Tuesday	Wednesday	Thursday	Friday	Saturday	Sunday
1)	화요일	2)	3)	금요일	토요일	4)

Answer 1) 월요일 2) 수요일 3) 목요일 4) 일요일

Telling the time when something happens (1)

TRACK 19

Grammar Points

N에

The particle '에' follows nouns which indicate time.

토요일에, 열 시에, 오 분에, 주말에, 오전에, 오후에, …

'에' is not used after '어제, 오늘, 내일'.

▶ Grammar Reference p.147

A 몇 시에 일어나요?
B 일곱 시에 일어나요.

A What time do you get up?
B I get up at 7 o'clock.

A 몇 시에 밥을 먹어요?
B 여덟 시쯤에 먹어요.

A What time do you eat your meal?
B I eat around 8 o'clock.

Notes

When telling numbers in approximation, '쯤' is added after the number.

Practice

Look at the pictures below, and practice the dialogue with your partner.

일어나다

밥을 먹다

친구를 만나다

자다

Telling the time when something happens (2)

TRACK 19

Notes

When saying that the same thing is done at a different time, '에도' is added after the time.
When emphasizing a particular time, '에는' is added after the time.

A 무슨 요일에 태권도를 배워요?

B 월요일에 태권도를 배워요.

A 화요일에도 태권도를 배워요?

B 아니요, 화요일에는 태권도를 안 배워요.

A On what day do you take taekwondo lessons?

B I take taekwondo lessons on Mondays.

A Do you take taekwondo lessons on Tuesdays, too?

B No, I don't take taekwondo lessons on Tuesdays.

Practice

Write '에' in the parentheses if needed, otherwise mark X.

1) 주말(　　) 영화를 봐요.
2) 오늘(　　) 뭐 해요?
3) 지금(　　) 책을 읽어요.
4) 무슨 요일(　　) 태권도를 배워요?

Answer 1) 에 2) × 3) × 4) 에

Expressing contrast

TRACK 19

Grammar Points

S-지만 S'

When two sentences show contrast in content, they can be connected by adding '-지만' to the stem of the verb or adjective of the preceding sentence.

▶ Grammar Reference p.147

A 내일 학교에 가요?

B 나는 학교에 가지만 애니 씨는 안 가요.

A Are you going to school tomorrow?

B I'm going to school but Annie isn't.

Practice

Link two sentences using '-지만'.

1) 나, 밥을 먹다 / 쿠마르 씨, 빵을 먹다

______________________________.

2) 나, 한국어를 공부하다 / 미사코 씨, 영어를 공부하다

______________________________.

3) 애니 씨, 백화점에 가다 / 크리스 씨, 시장에 가다

______________________________.

4) 바나나, 싸다 / 포도, 비싸다

______________________________.

Answer 1) 나는 밥을 먹지만 쿠마르 씨는 빵을 먹어요 2) 나는 한국어를 공부하지만 미사코 씨는 영어를 공부해요 3) 애니 씨는 백화점에 가지만 크리스 씨는 시장에 가요 4) 바나나는 싸지만 포도는 비싸요

Conversation Drills 대화 연습

Conversation 1

TRACK 20

A Sophia, what are you doing today?
B I'm going to school.
A What time do you go to school?
B I go to school at 10.

A 소피아 씨, 오늘 뭐 해요?

B 학교에 가요.

A 몇 시에 학교에 가요?

B 열 시에 학교에 가요.

Check it

소피아 씨는 몇 시에 학교에 가요?

① 8시 ② 10시

Answer ②

Practice the dialogue with your partner, using the following schedule.

1) | 학교에 가다 |
|---|
| 10시 |

2) | 애니 씨를 만나다 |
|---|
| 5시 |

3) | 영화를 보다 |
|---|
| 7시 |

Conversation 2

TRACK 20

A What do you do on Wednesdays, Lisa?

B On Wednesdays I go to school.

A Do you go to school on Thursdays, too?

B No, I go to school on Wednesdays but not on Thursdays.

A 리사 씨, 수요일에 뭐 해요?

B 수요일에는 학교에 가요.

A 목요일에도 학교에 가요?

B 아니요, 수요일에는 학교에 가지만 목요일에는 학교에 안 가요.

Check it

리사 씨는 목요일에 학교에 가요.

T F

Answer F

Practice the dialogue with your partner.

1)

수요일
학교 / 가다
목요일
수요일 O / 목요일 X

2)

월요일
태권도 / 배우다
화요일
월요일 O / 화요일 X

3)

금요일
재민 씨 / 만나다
토요일
금요일 O / 토요일 X

Tasks & Activities 과제

Pair work

Ask your partner about his/her daily routines below, and mark the time on the clock.

몇 시에 일어나요?

6시 30분에 일어나요.

일어나다

밥을 먹다

친구를 만나다

일하다

공부하다

텔레비전을 보다

샤워하다

?

______

?

______

Listening 듣기

TRACK 21

1. Listen to the following, and fill in the blanks.

1) _____시 _____분

2) _____시 _____분

3) _____시 _____분

4) _____시 _____분

2. Listen carefully, and match the time with the correct activity.

1) 5시 40분

2) 8시 20분

3) 7시 30분

4) 11시

①

②

③

④

⑤

3. **Listen carefully, and write down the number of the activity scheduled for each day.**

①

②

③

④

월요일	화요일	수요일	목요일	금요일	토요일	일요일

4. **Listen carefully, and complete the person's schedule.**

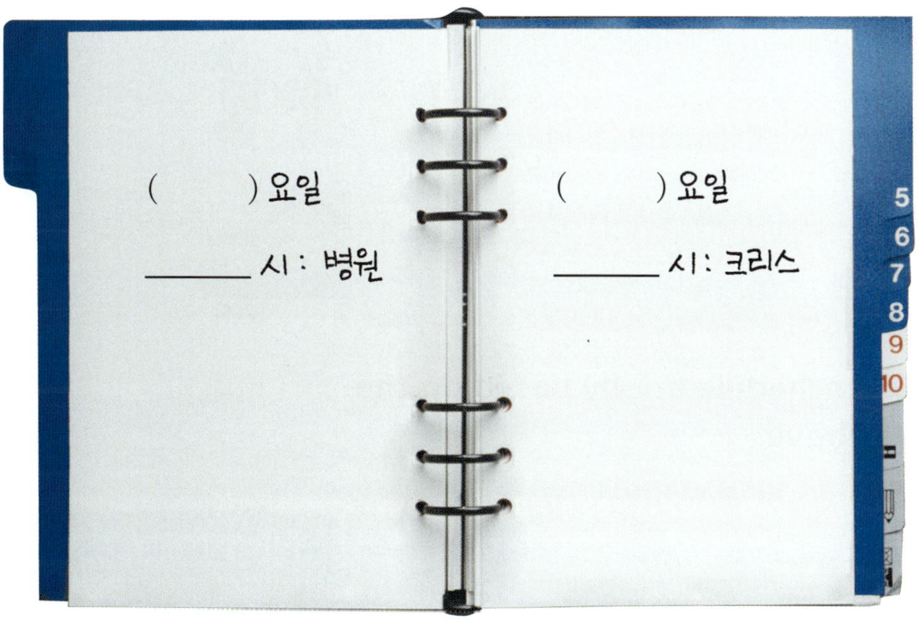

Answer 1. 1) 6시 20분 2) 2시 45분 3) 4시 30분 4) 9시 25분

2. 1) ⑤ 2) ② 3) ③ 4) ①

3.

월요일	화요일	수요일	목요일	금요일	토요일	일요일
①		③	④		②	

4. 토, 9, 일, 3

Reading & Writing 읽기와 쓰기

1. Match each day of the week with a correct picture.

> 오늘은 금요일이에요. 오늘 나는 학교에 가요. 그리고 한국어를 배워요. 내일은 학교에 안 가요. 오전에는 영어를 가르쳐요. 오후에는 시장에 가요. 일요일에는 친구를 만나요. 그리고 산에 가요.

1) 금요일 •

2) 토요일 •

3) 일요일 •

• ① 

• ② 

• ③ 

• ④ 

• ⑤ 

2. Write your daily schedule briefly based on the given example above.

Answer 1. 1) ② 2) ①, ③ 3) ④, ⑤

Now I can...

- ☐ talk about time
- ☐ talk about days of the week
- ☐ tell the time when something happens
- ☐ express contrast among several things

in Korean.

Additional Expressions 추가 표현

Words which indicate time

아침
morning

점심
midday
(around lunch time)

저녁
evening

밤
night

12:00

오전	오후
a.m.	p.m.

JULY 7월

월요일	화요일	수요일	목요일	금요일	토요일	일요일
1	2 그제 the day before yesterday	3 어제 yesterday	(4) 오늘 today	5 내일 tomorrow	6 모레 the day after tomorrow	7

UNIT 7

Appointment
약속

In This Unit

- Making suggestions 제안하기
- Talking about dates 날짜 말하기
- Making appointments 약속하기

Expressions 표현

시간이 있어요.	I have time.
시간이 없어요.	I don't have time.
오늘이 며칠이에요?	What's the date today?
어제 뭘 했어요?	What did you do yesterday?
그럼 책방 앞은 어때요?	How about in front of the bookstore?
토요일은 어때요?	How about Saturday?
좋아요.	Fine. / Good.

Vocabulary 어휘

Months

일월 January
이월 February
삼월 March
사월 April
오월 May
유월 June
칠월 July
팔월 August
구월 September
시월 October
십일월 November
십이월 December

Time

며칠 what date
월 month
일 day

Places

도서관 library
책방 bookstore
극장 movie theater
시청 city hall
커피숍 coffee shop

Others

수영하다 to swim
앞 front
점심 lunch
일본어 Japanese (language)
시험 test
생일 birthday
파티 party
추석 the Korean Thanksgiving
숙제하다 to do homework

Words that go together

시간이 있다 to have time
약속이 있다 to have an appointment
시험을 보다 to take a test

Key Dialogues 핵심 대화

Making suggestions

TRACK 22

A 산에 갈까요?

B 네, 좋아요.

A Shall we go to the mountain?

B Yes, that's fine.

A 내일 영화 볼까요?

B 내일은 시간이 없어요.

A Shall we see a movie tomorrow?

B I don't have time tomorrow.

Grammar Points

V-(으)ㄹ까요?

'-(으)ㄹ까요?' is used for suggestions.

verb stems ending with a vowel + -ㄹ까요? : 가다 → 갈까요?

verb stems ending with a consonant + -을까요? : 먹다 → 먹을까요?

As an answer to this pattern, 'V-아요/어요' can be used. In this case, 'V-아요/어요' has the meaning 'Let's~.'

▶ Grammar Reference p.147

Notes

When you have time (for something / to do something), you say "시간이 있어요." and "시간이 없어요." when you don't.

Practice

1 Change the words below using '-(으)ㄹ까요?'.

1) 보다 – (　　　　　)?　　2) 읽다 – (　　　　　)?

3) 먹다 – (　　　　　)?　　4) 만나다 – (　　　　　)?

2 Fill in the blanks with the correct answer.

1) **A** 뭘 먹을까요?

B 냉면을 (　　　　　).

2) **A** 몇 시에 만날까요?

B 세 시에 (　　　　　).

Answer **1** 1) 볼까요 2) 읽을까요 3) 먹을까요 4) 만날까요 **2** 1) 먹어요 2) 만나요

Giving the date

TRACK 22

A 오늘이 며칠이에요?

B 오늘은 시월 십칠 일이에요.

A What's the date today?

B Today is October 17.

Grammar Points

_월 _일

In Korean, when giving dates, the month comes first and then the date follows. For dates, we use the number system '일, 이, 삼, 사…'. Therefore, when saying the month, they will be '일월, 이월, 삼월, 사월' and so on, and when saying the dates '일 일, 이 일, 삼 일, 사 일' and so on. But there are spelling changes for '6월' and '10월', which become '유월' and '시월', respectively. When asking the date, '며칠' is used.

▶▶ Grammar Reference p.148

Practice

1 What is the correct word for the blank below?

A 오늘이 (   )이에요?

B 구월 삼 일이에요.

① 며칠　　② 무슨 요일

2 Look at the dates below and write them in Korean.

1) 10월 15일 – (   )

2) 8월 20일 – (   )

3) 6월 6일 – (   )

4) 4월 23일 – (   )

Answer **1** ① **2** 1) 시월 십오 일 2) 팔월 이십 일 3) 유월 육 일 4) 사월 이십삼 일

Talking about something you did in the past

TRACK 22

A 어제 뭘 했어요?

B 영어를 가르쳤어요.

A What did you do yesterday?

B I taught English.

Grammar Points

A/V-았어요/었어요

Adding '-았어요/었어요' to the stem of a verb or an adjective makes it past tense.

verb or adjective stem's last vowels ending with 'ㅏ' or 'ㅗ' + -았어요 : 가다 → 갔어요

verbs or adjectives ending with '하다' ➡ 했어요 : 공부하다 → 공부했어요

In all other cases, add '-었어요' : 가르치다 → 가르쳤어요

▶ Grammar Reference p.148

Practice

1 Change the following verbs into past tense.

1) 가다 – (　　　　)　2) 먹다 – (　　　　)　3) 공부하다 – (　　　　)

4) 마시다 – (　　　　)　5) 오다 – (　　　　)　6) 배우다 – (　　　　)

2 What did you do yesterday? Answer using the pictures below.

1)  책을 읽다

2)  커피를 마시다

3)  수영하다

4)  영화를 보다

5)  밥을 먹다

Answer **1** 1) 갔어요 2) 먹었어요 3) 공부했어요 4) 마셨어요 5) 왔어요 6) 배웠어요 **2** 1) 책을 읽었어요. 2) 커피를 마셨어요. 3) 수영했어요. 4) 영화를 봤어요. 5) 밥을 먹었어요.

Talking about places

TRACK 22

A 어디에서 만날까요?

B 도서관 앞에서 만나요.

A 도서관 앞은 복잡해요.

B 그럼 책방 앞은 어때요?

A Where shall we meet?

B Let's meet in front of the library.

A It's crowded in front of the library.

B Then how about in front of the bookstore?

Grammar Points

N에서

'에서' is a particle that indicates the place where the action of the verb phrase takes place.

▶ Grammar Reference p.149

Notes

When making follow-up suggestions, you say '그럼 ~은/는 어때요?'

Practice

1 Complete the sentences using '에/에서'.

1) 지금 어디(　　　) 가요?　　2) 저는 도서관(　　　) 책을 읽어요.

3) 몇 시(　　　) 만날까요?　　4) 식당(　　　) 점심을 먹어요.

2 Make sentences about what you can do at the following places.

극장에서 영화를 봐요.

극장

백화점

학교

산

식당

Answer **1** 1) 에 2) 에서 3) 에 4) 에서

Conversation Drills 대화 연습

Conversation 1

TRACK 23

A 민수 씨, 내일 영화 볼까요?

B 내일은 시간이 없어요.

A 그럼 토요일은 어때요?

B 좋아요.

A Minsu, shall we see a movie tomorrow?

B I don't have time tomorrow.

A Then how about Saturday?

B Sounds good.

Check it

1. 민수 씨는 내일 영화를 봐요.
   T F

2. 민수 씨는 토요일에 시간이 있어요.
   T F

Answer 1. F 2. T

Practice the dialogue with your partner.

1) 내일 / 영화 보다
   내일 / 시간이 없다
   토요일

2) 시청 앞 / 만나다
   시청 앞 / 복잡하다
   서울책방

3) 토요일 / 공원에 가다
   토요일 / 약속이 있다
   일요일

Conversation 2

TRACK 23

A Shall we see a movie on Saturday?

B What date is this Saturday?

A It is May 3.

B Fine. What time shall we meet?

A Let's meet at 2 in front of the school.

B Alright.

A 토요일에 영화 볼까요?

B 토요일이 며칠이에요?

A 5월 3일이에요.

B 좋아요. 몇 시에 만날까요?

A 2시에 학교 앞에서 만나요.

B 좋아요.

Check it

1. 두 사람은 5월 3일에 영화를 봐요.
   T F

2. 두 사람은 2시에 밥을 먹어요.
   T F

Answer 1. T 2. F

Practice the dialogue with your partner.

1)

토요일 / 영화 보다
토요일
5월 3일
몇 시
2시

2)

일요일 / 산에 가다
일요일
8월 26일
몇 시
8시 반

3)

목요일 / 수영하다
목요일
10월 20일
몇 시
10시

Tasks & Activities 과제

Pair work

You would like to go to the movies with your friend. Find out when your friend has time and make an appointment.

A		
일	9:00 a.m.	산
월		
화	7:00 p.m.	친구 생일 (햄버거킹)
수	2:20 p.m.	태권도
목		
금	4:30 p.m.	시장
토		

B		
일		
월	10:00 a.m.	일본어 공부
화		
수	1:00 p.m.	시험
목	3:00 p.m.	친구 (하나커피숍)
금		
토	9:30 a.m.	일본

Listening 듣기

TRACK 24

1. Listen carefully, and write down the correct date.

1) _____월 _____일　　2) _____월 _____일

3) _____월 _____일　　4) _____월 _____일

5) _____월 _____일　　6) _____월 _____일

2. Listen carefully, and connect each picture with the correct date.

1) 

2) 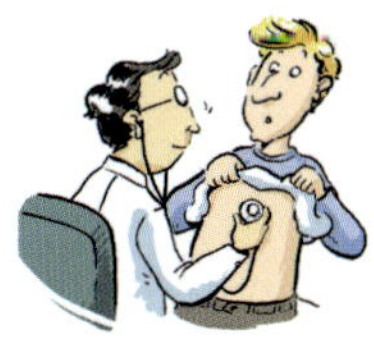

3) 

4) 

5) 

6) 

5월

일	월	화	수	목	금	토
	1	2	3	4	5	6
7	8	9	10	11	12	13
14	15	16	17	18	19	20
21	22	23	24	25	26	27
28	29	30	31			

3. Circle the correct answer.

1) 두 사람은 (토요일 / 일요일)에 영화를 봐요.

2) 미사코 씨는 영화 '집으로'를 (봤어요 / 안 봤어요).

3) 두 사람은 (2시 / 3시)에 극장 앞에서 만나요.

Answer **1.** 1) 11월 20일 2) 10월 15일 3) 9월 13일 4) 2월 8일 5) 6월 4일 6) 8월 27일

2. 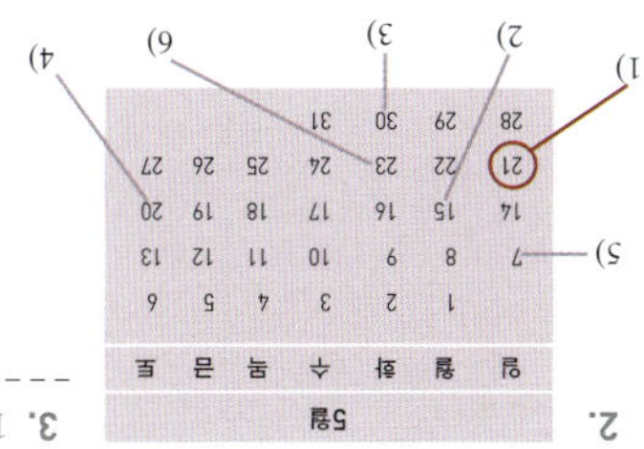

3. 1) 일요일 2) 안 봤어요 3) 2시

Reading & Writing 읽기와 쓰기

1. The following is Andy's schedule. Mark O if it is correct, and mark X if it is incorrect.

July

월	화	수	목	금	토	일
3	4 태권도 (14:00 ~15:00)	5 친구 생일 파티 (18:00~)	6	7 시험 (09:00 ~11:00)	⑧ 오늘	9 영화 (11:30~) 한국극장

1) 앤디 씨는 칠월 사 일에 태권도를 배웠어요. ( )

2) 앤디 씨는 칠월 삼 일에 시험을 봤어요. ( )

3) 일요일에 앤디 씨는 한국극장에서 영화를 봐요. ( )

4) 앤디 씨는 목요일에 약속이 없어요. ( )

2. What did you do yesterday? Write about what you did yesterday.

나는 어제 ______ 시에 일어났어요. ____

____

____

____

____

Now I can...

- ☐ make a suggestion
- ☐ talk about dates
- ☐ make an appointment

in Korean.

Answer 1. 1) O 2) X 3) O 4) O

Additional Expressions 추가 표현

Places

우체국 post office

백화점 department store

커피숍 coffee shop

서점 bookstore

극장 theater

도서관 library

은행 bank

식당 restaurant

노래방 singing room (furnished with karaoke)

PC방 internet cafe

미장원 beauty shop

공원 park

UNIT 8

Locations & Directions

위치와 방향

In This Unit

- Asking for and giving locations 위치 묻고 대답하기
- Asking for and giving directions 길 묻고 대답하기

Expressions 표현

책이 어디에 있어요?	Where is the book? / Where are the books?
이 근처에 세탁소가 있어요?	Is there a dry cleaner's around here?
앞으로 쭉 가세요.	Go straight forward.
얼마나 걸려요?	How long does it take?
고맙습니다. / 감사합니다.	Thank you.

Vocabulary 어휘

Locations / Positions

위 above / on
아래 under / below
앞 front
뒤 behind
옆 beside / side
안 inside
오른쪽 right side
왼쪽 left side

Places

방 room
세탁소 dry cleaner's
서울대학교 Seoul National University
교실 classroom
지하철역 subway station
가게 store / shop
우체국 post office
약국 pharmacy
은행 bank
화장실 rest room
호텔 hotel

Furniture & Home appliances

컴퓨터 computer
옷장 wardrobe / closet
냉장고 refrigerator
책상 desk
침대 bed
소파 sofa
의자 chair

Nouns

층 floor
버스 bus
시간 hour
생선 fish
술 liquor
야채 vegetable
과일 fruit
아이스크림 ice cream
코트 coat

Others

걸리다 to take (time)

Key Dialogues 핵심 대화

Asking whether an item exists or not

TRACK 25

A 방에 컴퓨터가 있어요?

B 네, 있어요.

A Do you have a computer in your room?

B Yes, I do.

Grammar Points

N이/가 N'에 있다/없다

'N이/가 있어요' means that N is located or exists, while 'N이/가 없어요' means the opposite. 'N'에' is used with 'N이/가 있어요' to show where N is located.

▶ Grammar Reference p.149

A 방에 옷장이 있어요?

B 아니요, 없어요.

A Do you have a closet in your room?

B No, I don't.

Practice

Ask your partner if he/she has the following items.

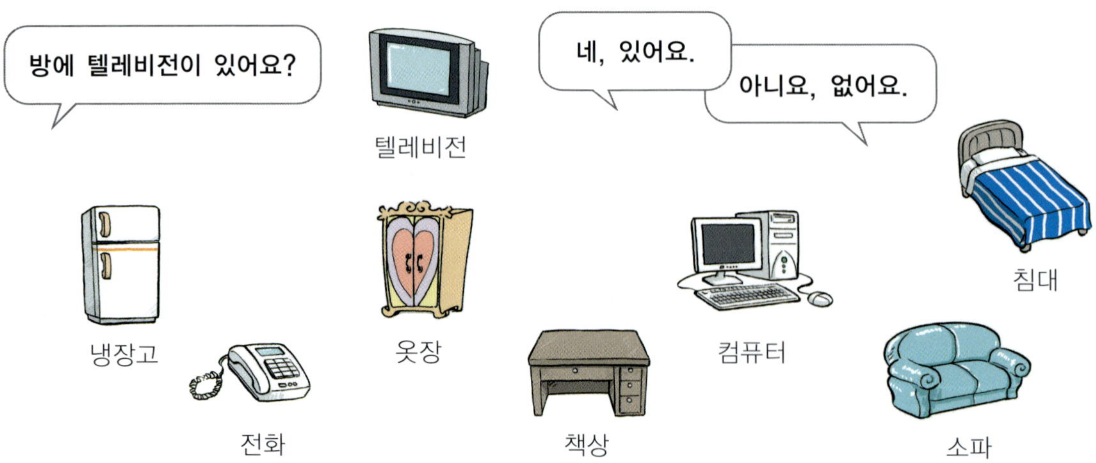

Giving the location of an item

TRACK 25

A 책이 어디에 있어요?

B 책상 위에 있어요.

A Where is the book?

B It's on the desk.

Grammar Points

N 위/아래/앞/뒤/옆/안에

Words that denote position such as '위, 아래, 앞, etc.' come after the noun that become the basis for the direction.

의자 [위 / 아래 / 앞 / 뒤 / 옆 / 안] 에 있어요.

▶ Grammar Reference p.149

Practice

1 Connect each word with the correct picture.

1) 앞 2) 뒤 3) 위 4) 옆

① 

② 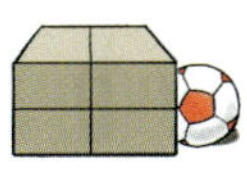

③ 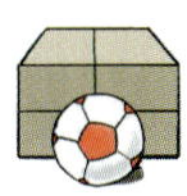

④ 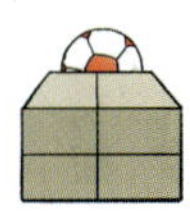

2 Mark O if the sentences below match the picture, and mark X if not.

1) 책이 침대 위에 있어요. ( )
2) 시계가 의자 옆에 있어요. ( )
3) 휴대 전화가 의자 아래에 있어요. ( )
4) 책상이 침대 옆에 있어요. ( )

Answer 1 1) ③ 2) ④ 3) ① 4) ② 2 1) O 2) X 3) X 4) O

Asking for and giving locations

TRACK 25

A 식당이 몇 층에 있어요?

B 삼 층에 있어요.

A What floor is the restaurant on?

B It's on the third floor.

A 이 근처에 세탁소가 있어요?

B 네, 있어요.

A Is there a dry cleaner's around here?

B Yes, there is.

Notes

When talking about on what floor something is located, '층', which means 'floor', is added after the number.

1층 → 일 층
2층 → 이 층
3층 → 삼 층
⋮

Notes

When asking if there is a specific place around the area, you say "이 근처에 N이/가 있어요?"

Asking for and giving directions

TRACK 25

A 이 버스는 서울대학교로 가요?

B 네, 가요.

A Does this bus go to Seoul National University?

B Yes, it does.

Grammar Points

N(으)로 가다/오다

Used after a place noun, '(으)로' indicates the direction toward that place.

nouns ending with a vowel + 로 : 서울대학교 → 서울대학교로

nouns ending with a consonant + 으로 : 앞 → 앞으로

nouns ending with 'ㄹ' + '로' : 교실 → 교실로

▶ Grammar Reference p.150

Practice

1 Connect each sign with the correct meaning.

1)  •   • ① 앞으로 가세요.

2)  •   • ② 오른쪽으로 가세요.

3)  •   • ③ 왼쪽으로 가세요.

2 Circle the correct particle.

1) 뒤(로 / 으로) 가요.
2) 한국(로 / 으로) 왔어요.
3) 옆(로 / 으로) 오세요.
4) 교실(로 / 으로) 갈까요?

Answer **1** 1) ③ 2) ① 3) ② **2** 1) 로 2) 으로 3) 으로 4) 로

Asking how long it takes to the destination

TRACK 25

A 지하철역까지 얼마나 걸려요?

B 십 분쯤 걸려요.

A How long does it take to get to the subway station?

B It takes about 10 minutes.

Grammar Points

N까지

'까지' after a place noun means 'until the end of a certain range.'

▶ Grammar Reference p.150

Grammar Points

분, 시간

When talking about the time to do something, use '분' for minutes and '시간' for hours.

▶ Grammar Reference p.150

Practice

Pair up, and ask your partner how long it takes to the following places.

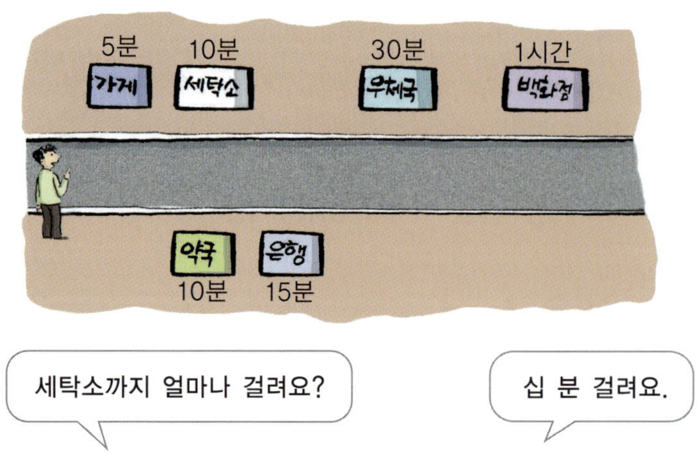

Conversation Drills 대화 연습

Conversation 1

TRACK 26

A Where are the fish?

B Go straight to the left.
It is next to the meat store.

A Where are the juice?

B Go straight forward. They're next to the liquor section.

A 생선이 어디에 있어요?

B 왼쪽으로 쭉 가세요. 생선은 고기 가게 옆에 있어요.

A 주스는 어디에 있어요?

B 앞으로 쭉 가세요. 술 옆에 있어요.

Check it

1. 생선 가게는 없어요.
   T F

2. 주스는 술 옆에 있어요.
   T F

Answer 1. F 2. T

Practice the dialogue with your partner.

1)	2)	3)	4)
생선	야채	고기	술
왼쪽 / 생선, 고기 가게	오른쪽 / 야채, 과일	왼쪽 / 고기, 생선 가게	앞 / 술, 콜라
주스	우유	과일	아이스크림
앞 / 술	앞 / 주스	오른쪽 / 야채	오른쪽 / 치즈

Conversation 2

TRACK 26

A Is there a department store around here?

B Yes, there is. Go straight this way. Then it is on the right.

A How long does it take?

B It takes about 10 minutes.

A Thank you.

A 이 근처에 백화점이 있어요?

B 네, 있어요. 이쪽으로 쭉 가세요. 그럼 오른쪽에 있어요.

A 얼마나 걸려요?

B 10분쯤 걸려요.

A 고맙습니다.

Check it

1. 이 근처에 백화점이 있어요. T F
2. 백화점까지 십오 분쯤 걸려요. T F

Answer 1. T 2. F

Practice the dialogue with your partner.

	1)	2)	3)	4)
	백화점	우체국	세탁소	은행
	오른쪽 / 10분	왼쪽 / 10분	오른쪽 / 5분	왼쪽 / 5분

Tasks & Activities 과제

Pair work

Part A

Ask your partner where the items in the box are. And then write down the number for each item in the picture below. Your partner will answer the questions with the information provided on the next page.

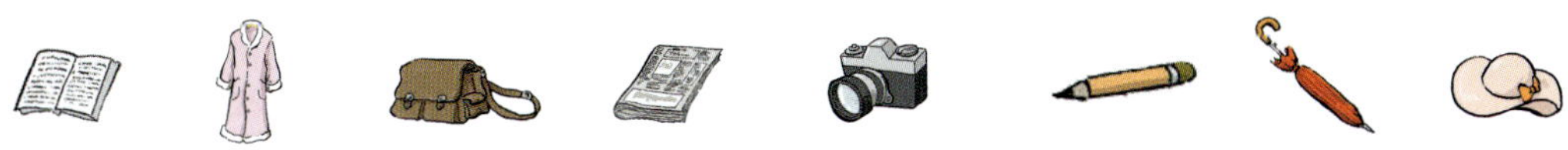

① 책 ② 코트 ③ 가방 ④ 신문 ⑤ 카메라 ⑥ 연필 ⑦ 우산 ⑧ 모자

Part B

Answer the questions from Part A using the picture below.

Listening 듣기

TRACK 27

1. Listen carefully, and connect each picture with the correct floor of the department store.

1) 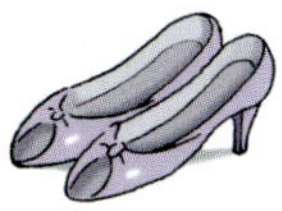

2) 

3) 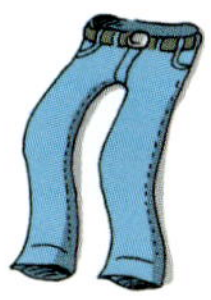

4) 

5) 

6) 

2. **Listen to the dialogue, and write down the number of the place where the following item is located.**

1)  __________

2)  __________

3)  __________

4)  __________

3. **Listen to the dialogue, and write down the number of each building the person is looking for.**

1) __________

2) __________

3) __________

Answer **1.** 1) 4층 2) 1층 3) 2층 4) 7층 5) 9층 6) 9층
2. 1) ③ 2) ① 3) ⑤ 4) ⑥ **3.** 1) ③ 2) ② 3) ①

Reading & Writing 읽기와 쓰기

1. Read the following passage, and match the place with the item(s).

여기는 제 방이에요. 제 방에는 침대하고 책상하고 의자가 있어요. 침대 위에 가방이 있어요. 그리고 책상 위에 컴퓨터하고 책이 있어요. 저는 제 방에서 컴퓨터를 해요. 의자 옆에 구두가 있어요. 텔레비전하고 냉장고는 제 방에 없어요.

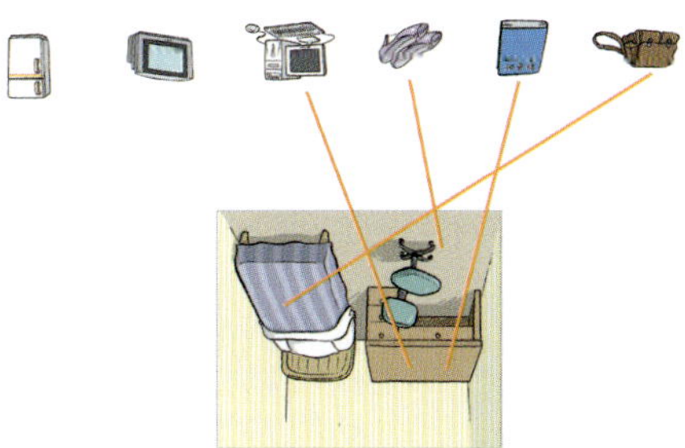

Answer 1.

2. Look at the picture below, and describe the room.

여기는 제 방이에요.

Now I can...

- ☐ ask for and give locations
- ☐ ask for and give directions

in Korean.

Additional Expressions 추가 표현

Giving directions

육교를 건너세요.
Use the overpass.

횡단보도를 건너세요.
Use the crosswalk.

지하도를 건너세요.
Use the underpass.

첫 번째 사거리에서 오른쪽으로 가세요.
Turn right at the first crossroad.

쭉 가다가 왼쪽으로 가세요.
Go straight and then turn left.

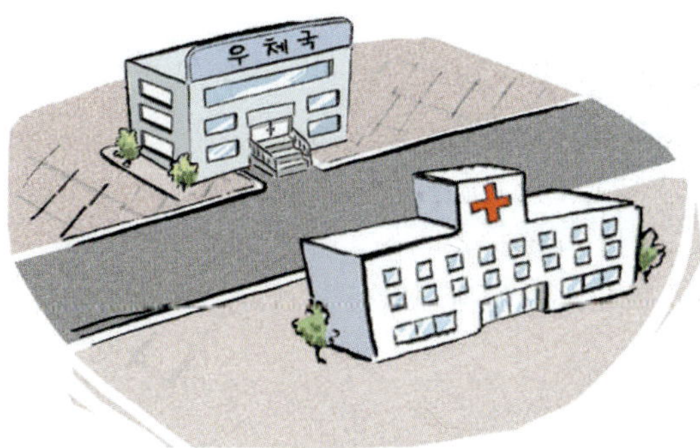

우체국은 병원 건너편에 있어요.
The post office is across from the hospital.

UNIT 9

Phone Call

전화

In This Unit

- Making phone calls 전화하기
- Confirming 확인하기
- Making requests (2) 요청하기 (2)

Expressions 표현

여보세요.	Hello.
거기 애니 씨 집이지요?	Is this Annie's house?
네, 그런데요.	Yes, it is.
실례지만 누구세요?	Excuse me, but may I ask who is calling?
재민 씨 좀 바꿔 주세요.	Can I talk to Jaemin, please?
네, 알겠습니다.	Okay, I see.
소피아 씨, 전화 받으세요.	Sophia, you've got a phone call.

Vocabulary 어휘

Verbs

바꾸다 to change	전화하다 to call	회의하다 to hold a meeting	춤추다 to dance
받다 to receive / to take / to get	만들다 to make	노래하다 to sing	열다 to open
	준비하다 to prepare	그리다 to draw / to paint	닫다 to close

Nouns

케이크 cake	그림 picture / drawing	문 door	저녁 evening
음식 food	창문 window	부엌 kitchen	

Others

가위바위보 rock, paper, scissors

아직 (not) yet, still

빨리 quickly

Words that go together

전화를 받다 to get (answer) the telephone

그림을 그리다 to draw a picture

Key Dialogues 핵심 대화

Asking if you called the right number

TRACK 28

A 여보세요. 거기 애니 씨 집이지요?

B 네, 그런데요. 실례지만 누구세요?

A Hello. This is Annie's house, isn't it?

B Yes, it is. Excuse me, but may I ask who's calling?

Grammar Points

N-(이)지요?

'-(이)지요' expresses either a) the speaker's strong conviction about a certain fact or state of affairs or b) that the fact or state of affairs referred to is something already known to both the speaker and listener.

nouns ending with a vowel + -지요? : 의사 → 의사지요?

nouns ending with a consonant + -이지요? : 목요일 → 목요일이지요?

▶ Grammar Reference p.150

Notes

"여보세요." means "Hello," and is used when calling or answering a phone call.

Notes

When asking who is calling, you say "실례지만 누구세요?"

Practice

Circle the correct sentence ending.

1) 재민 씨는 학생(지요 / 이지요)?
2) 저 사람이 애니 씨(지요 / 이지요)?
3) 내일은 수요일(지요 / 이지요)?
4) 안나 씨는 요리사(지요 / 이지요)?

Answer 1) 이지요 2) 지요 3) 이지요 4) 지요

Putting someone on the phone

TRACK 28

A 애니 씨 좀 바꿔 주세요.

B 네, 잠깐만 기다리세요.

애니 씨, 전화 받으세요.

A Can I talk to Annie, please?

B Yes, just a moment.

Annie, you've got a phone call.

Grammar Points

V–아/어 주세요

'–아/어 주세요' is a polite form of requesting for help, assistance, etc. '–아/어 주세요' has a meaning that the requested action is beneficial to the speaker or the receiver of the act.

verb stem's last vowels ending with 'ㅏ' or 'ㅗ' + –아 주세요 : 오다 → 와 주세요

verbs ending with '하다', 하다 → 해 주세요 : 전화하다 → 전화해 주세요

In all other cases, add '–어 주세요' : 바꾸다 → 바꿔 주세요

▶ Grammar Reference p.151

Practice

Complete the following sentences using '–아/어 주세요' pattern and the words given in the parentheses.

1) 책을 ______________________________. (사다)

2) 케이크를 ___________________________. (만들다)

3) 내일 ______________________________. (오다)

4) 음식을 _____________________________. (준비하다)

Answer 1) 사 주세요 2) 만들어 주세요 3) 와 주세요 4) 준비해 주세요

Expressing an action in progress

TRACK 28

Grammar Points

V-고 있다

Adding '-고 있다' to a verb stem shows the action is in progress.

자다 → 자고 있어요

▶ Grammar Reference p.151

A 재민 씨 좀 바꿔 주세요.
B 지금 자고 있어요.
A 네, 알겠습니다. 안녕히 계세요.

A Can I talk to Jaemin, please?
B He is sleeping now.
A Okay, I see. Good-bye.

Practice

Change the following verbs into '-고 있어요' pattern.

자다 → 자고 있어요

1) 먹다 →
2) 읽다 →
3) 쉬다 →
4) 일하다 →

Answer 1) 먹고 있어요 2) 읽고 있어요 3) 쉬고 있어요 4) 일하고 있어요

Conversation Drills 대화 연습

Conversation 1

TRACK 29

A Hello. Is this Sophia's house?

B Yes, that's right. Excuse me but who is calling, please?

A This is Seonwoo.

B Please wait a moment. Sophia, you've got a phone call.

A 여보세요. 거기 소피아 씨 집이지요?

B 네, 그런데요. 실례지만 누구세요?

A 저는 선우예요.

B 잠깐만 기다리세요.
소피아 씨, 전화 받으세요.

Check it

1. 선우 씨가 전화했어요.
   T F

2. 소피아 씨는 집에 없어요.
   T F

Answer 1. T 2. F

Practice the dialogue with your partner.

1)	2)	3)	4)
소피아	미사코	소피아	올가
선우	올리버	애니	마이클

Conversation 2

TRACK 29

A Hello, is this Peter's house?

B Yes, that's right.

A May I talk to Peter, please?

B He is taking a shower at the moment.

A Okay, I see. Good-bye.

A 여보세요, 피터 씨 집이지요?

B 네, 그런데요.

A 피터 씨 좀 바꿔 주세요.

B 지금 샤워하고 있어요.

A 네, 알겠습니다. 안녕히 계세요.

Check it

피터 씨는 지금 뭐 해요?

☐ 샤워해요.

☐ 전화해요.

Answer ✓ 샤워해요.

Practice the dialogue with your partner.

1) 피터 씨 집
피터 씨

샤워하다

2) 애니 씨 집
애니 씨

자다

3) 서울컴퓨터
재민 씨

회의하다

Tasks & Activities 과제

Pair work

Let's play rock, paper, scissors. The winner chooses one of the pictures below and asks the other person to perform the task in the picture. When you ask, you should use the pattern '-아/어 주세요'. The loser must do what he/she has been asked. If the winner cannot make a correct sentence, the loser gets to choose.

노래하다

그림을 그리다

책을 읽다

춤추다

창문을 열다

숙제하다

전화하다

문을 닫다

커피를 사다

가위바위보

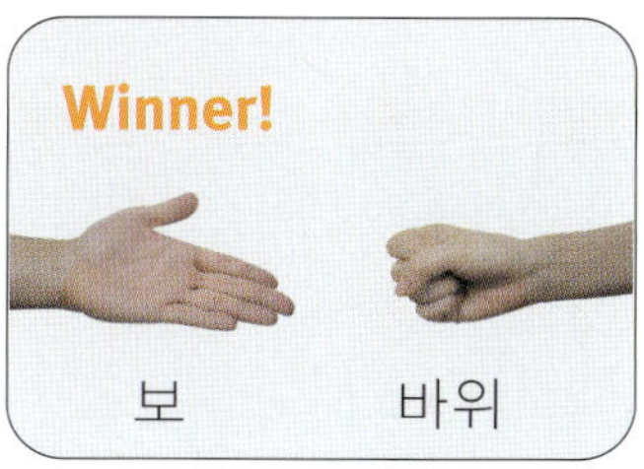

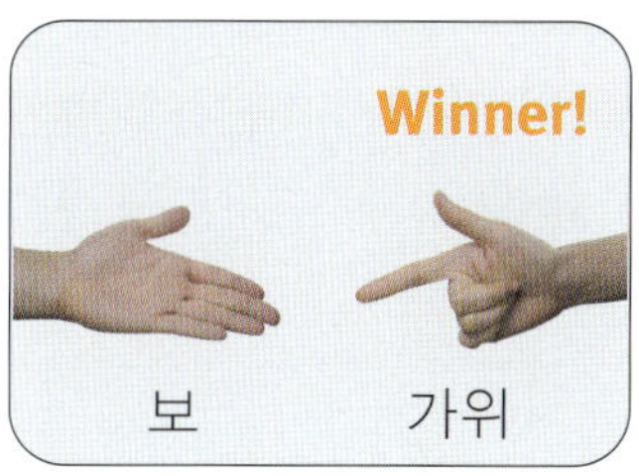

Listening 듣기

TRACK 30

1. Listen to the dialogue carefully. If the caller made the right call, mark O, and if the caller made the wrong call, mark X.

1) 재민 ________ 2) 크리스 ________

3) 서울대학교 ________

2. Saturday is Annie's birthday. Jaemin is organizing a party for Annie. Listen carefully, and match each person with the thing he/she should prepare.

1) 웨이 ●

2) 크리스 ●

3) 알렉스 ●

4) 미사코 ●

① 

② 

③ 

④ 

⑤ 

3. Listen to the dialogue, and mark O if it is correct, and mark X if it is incorrect.

1) 재민 씨가 전화했어요. (　　)
2) 크리스 씨가 전화를 받았어요. (　　)
3) 재민 씨는 도서관에 있어요. (　　)

Answer 1. 1) O 2) O 3) X 2. 1) ④ 2) ③ 3) ① 4) ② 3. 1) X 2) X 3) O

Reading & Writing 읽기와 쓰기

1. **There is a party at Michael's house. Read the following paragraph carefully, and write down the name of each person next to the matching picture.**

> 오늘 마이클 씨 집에서 파티를 해요. 재민 씨는 노래하고 있어요. 애니 씨는 주스를 마시고 있어요. 크리스 씨는 애니 씨 옆에 있어요. 신문을 보고 있어요. 마이클 씨는 부엌에 있어요. 음식을 준비하고 있어요. 미사코 씨는 아직 안 왔어요.

Answer 1. ①재민 ②애니 ③크리스

2. **Annie called Misako's house because Misako didn't show up, but the answering machine picked up. Write down a message for Misako.**

Now I can...

- ☐ make a phone call
- ☐ make expressions of confirmation
- ☐ make a request

in Korean.

Additional Expressions 추가 표현

Asking for and giving phone numbers

전화번호 좀 가르쳐 주세요.
Please tell me your phone number.

823-5760(팔이삼의 오칠육공)이에요.
It's eight two three five seven six zero.

• The pronunciation of '의', which corresponds to '–', is [에].

Asking if it is alright to talk on the phone now

지금 전화 괜찮아요?
Is it alright to talk on the phone now?

네, 괜찮아요.
Yes, it's alright.

Useful phone numbers in Korea

- 114 Telephone directory
- 112 Police emergency
- 119 Fire emergency
- 131 Weather information
- 116 Current time
- 1330 Tourist information

Grammar Reference 문법 설명

UNIT 2 Greetings & Introductions

1. N은/는

'은/는' follows a noun, indicating that it is the topic under discussion. The topic is often, but not necessarily, the same as the subject.

If the noun ends with a vowel + 는 : 저 → 저는
If the noun ends with a consonant + 은 : 이분 → 이분은

• 토니는 • 마이클은

2. N-이에요/예요

'-이에요/예요' are sentence endings expressing identification and are attached to nouns.

If the noun ends with a vowel + -예요 :
애니 → 애니예요
If the noun ends with a consonant + -이에요 :
학생 → 학생이에요

저는 애니예요.	I am Annie.
크리스 씨는 선생님이에요.	Chris is a teacher.

When using the '-이에요/예요' pattern, just raising the intonation at the end without any change in word order makes the sentence a question.

한국 사람이에요. ↘	I am Korean.
한국 사람이에요? ↗	Are you Korean?

3. 네, 아니요

For questions using the 'N-이에요/예요?' patterns, you answer using '네' or '아니요'.

A : 한국 사람이에요? B : 네, 한국 사람이에요.	Are you Korean? Yes, I'm Korean.
A : 한국 사람이에요? B : 아니요. 중국 사람이에요.	Are you Korean? No. I'm Chinese.

UNIT 3 Restaurant

1. V-(으)세요

'-(으)세요' is used to make requests, suggestions, or commands politely.

If the verb stem ends with a vowel + -세요 :
주다 → 주세요
If the verb stem ends with a consonant + -으세요 :
읽다 → 읽으세요

주세요.	Please give.
쓰세요.	Please write.
읽으세요.	Please read.

2. N 주세요

Adding '주세요' after N means requesting N for the speaker.

김밥 주세요.	Give me gimbap, please.
사과 주세요.	Give me some apples, please.

3. 하나, 둘, 셋, 넷, ···

'하나, 둘, 셋, 넷, ···' is the Korean numbering system. This is used for counting people or things in Korean.

1	2	3	4	5
하나	둘	셋	넷	다섯
6	7	8	9	10
여섯	일곱	여덟	아홉	열

'하나, 둘, 셋, 넷, ···' are added after the counted noun.
하나 사과 (X) → 사과 하나 (O)

사과 하나 주세요.	Please give me one apple.
오렌지 둘 주세요.	Please give me two oranges.
커피 셋 주세요.	Please give me three cups of coffee.

4. 병, 개, 잔

'병, 개, 잔' are counting units. In Korean, there is a variety of counting units to count objects. '개' is used widely to count general inanimate items, '병' for bottles and '잔' for cups or glasses.
When numbers and counting units are used together, numbers take different forms. Without counting units, they are '하나, 둘, 셋, 넷' but with counting units, they take the forms '한, 두, 세, 네'. The same rule applies to higher numbers such as '열하나, 열둘, 열셋, 열넷'.

1	한	병 · 개 · 잔
2	두	
3	세	
4	네	
5	다섯	
6	여섯	
7	일곱	
8	여덟	
9	아홉	
10	열	
11	열한	
12	열두	

The word order is as follows: items to be continued, numbers and counting units.

Items to be counted		Numbers	Counting units
사과		한	개
오렌지		두	개
콜라		세	병
커피		네	잔

'몇' means 'how many', and it forms a question when combined with counting units.

몇 개 how many (apples...)
몇 병 how many bottles of (beer...)
몇 잔 how many cups of (coffee...)

사과 한 개 주세요.	Please give me an apple.
콜라 두 병 주세요	Please give me two bottles of cola.
커피 세 잔 주세요.	Please give me three cups of coffee.
A : 몇 개예요? B : 네 개예요.	How many are there? Four.

5. N하고 N'

'하고' is used to connect two nouns with the meaning 'and'.

커피하고 녹차

빵하고 우유

커피하고 녹차 주세요. Please give me coffee and green tea.
빵하고 우유 주세요. Please give me some bread and milk.
냉면 둘하고 콜라 한 병 주세요. Please give me two bowls of naengmyeon and a bottle of cola.

UNIT 4 Shopping

1. N이/가 있어요/없어요

'N이/가 있어요' means the subject has N, and 'N이/가 없어요' means the subject doesn't have N.

돈이 있어요. 돈이 없어요.

If the noun ends with a vowel +가 : 시계 → 시계가
If the noun ends with a consonant +이 : 우산 → 우산이

시계가 있어요.	I have a watch.
우산이 없어요.	I don't have an umbrella.

'이' and '가' can be omitted in spoken Korean.

카메라(가) 있어요.	I have a camera.
돈(이) 없어요.	I don't have money.

Raising the intonation at the end without any changes in word order makes the sentence a question.

A : 우산이 있어요?	Do you have an umbrella?
B : 네, 있어요.	Yes, I do.

2. 이거, 그거, 저거

'이거, 그거, 저거' are used to point at things.
'이거' is used to point at the thing close to the speaker.
'그거' is used to point at the thing close to the listener.
'저거' is used to point at the thing away from both the speaker and the listener.

이거는 우유예요.	This is milk.
그거는 사전이에요.	That is a dictionary.
저거는 책이에요?	Is that a book?

'이거, 그거, 저거' are colloquial forms of '이것, 저것, 그것'.

이거 ← 이것
그거 ← 그것
저거 ← 저것

3. 이 N, 그 N, 저 N

'이, 그, 저' are always followed by a noun and used to point at things or people.
'이 N' indicates a thing or person close to the speaker.
'그 N' indicates a thing or person close to the listener.
'저 N' indicates a thing or person away from both the speaker and the listener.

이 시계는 제 시계예요.	This watch is my watch.
그 책은 한국어 책이에요.	That book is a Korean book.
저 사람은 재민 씨예요.	That person is Jaemin.

4. 일, 이, 삼, 사,…

For money, the following numbering system is used.

1	일	11	십일	30	삼십
2	이	12	십이	40	사십

3	삼	13	십삼	50	오십
4	사	14	십사	60	육십
5	오	15	십오	70	칠십
6	육	16	십육	80	팔십
7	칠	17	십칠	90	구십
8	팔	18	십팔	100	백
9	구	19	십구	1,000	천
10	십	20	이십	10,000	만

For prices, '원' (the Korean monetary unit) is used. There are 7 monetary denominations.

10원	50원	100원	500원
십 원	오십 원	백 원	오백 원

1,000원	5,000원	10,000원
천 원	오천 원	만 원

이 볼펜은 천팔백 원이에요.
This ball-point pen is 1,800 won.

A : 이 가방은 얼마예요? How much is this bag?
B : 삼만 오천 원이에요. It's 35,000 won.

UNIT 5 Daily Life

1. A/V-아요/어요

'-아요/어요' are casual sentence endings and make present tense verbs and adjectives.

If the verb or adjective stem's last vowel ends with 'ㅏ' or 'ㅗ' + -아요 : 만나다 → 만나요
If the verb or adjective ends with '하다', 하다 → 해요 : 좋아하다 → 좋아해요
In all other cases, add '-어요' : 먹다 → 먹어요

-아요
사다 → 사요
가다 → 가요
만나다 → 만나요
보다 → 봐요
오다 → 와요
좋다 → 좋아요
싸다 → 싸요

-해요
하다 → 해요
좋아하다 → 좋아해요
공부하다 → 공부해요
일하다 → 일해요
운동하다 → 운동해요
따뜻하다 → 따뜻해요
복잡하다 → 복잡해요

-어요
먹다 → 먹어요
읽다 → 읽어요
마시다 → 마셔요
가르치다 → 가르쳐요
배우다 → 배워요
맛있다 → 맛있어요
재미있다 → 재미있어요

Raising the intonation toward the end makes the sentence a question.
좋아요. ↘ → 좋아요? ↗

2. N을/를

'을/를' are attached to the end of a noun to make it the direct object of the verb.

If the noun ends with a vowel + 를 : 친구 → 친구를
If the noun ends with a consonant + 을 : 밥 → 밥을

The basic Korean word order is 'subject-object-verb.'

저는	사과를	먹어요.
subject	object	verb

Interrogative '뭐' and object marker '를' are often shortened into '뭘'.
뭐 + 를 → 뭘

Object particles are often omitted in spoken Korean.

애니 씨는 사과를 사요.	Annie buys apples.
재민 씨는 밥을 먹어요.	Jaemin eats his meal.
A : 뭘 읽어요? B : 책 읽어요.	What are you reading? I'm reading a book.

3. N에 가다/오다

'가다' is used when one is going away from the place where the conversation is taking place.
'오다' is used when one is coming toward the place where the conversation is taking place.

To show the destination, '에' is added after the place.

저는 학교에 가요.	I go to school.
우리 집에 오세요.	Come to my house, please.
A : 어디에 가요? B : 식당에 가요.	Where are you going? I'm going to a restaurant.

4. 안 A/V

The negating adverb '안' comes before a verb or an adjective and marks negation.

안 사요
안 먹어요

The verb '공부하다' consists of two parts, which are '공부(study)' and '하다(to do)'. In this case '안' ought to come right in front of '하다'. The same rule applies to these kind of verbs such as '일하다, 운동하다'.

안 공부해요 (X) → 공부 안 해요 (O)

저는 학교에 안 가요.	I don't go to school.
애니 씨는 고기를 안 먹어요.	Annie doesn't eat meat.
A : 재민 씨, 오늘 운동해요? Jaemin, are you going to work out today? B : 아니요, 운동 안 해요.	 No, I'm not.

5. N이/가 A

The subject marker '이 / 가' is attached to a noun to indicate that it is the subject of the sentence.

If the noun ends with a vowel + 가 : 김치 → 김치가
If the noun ends with a consonant + 이 : 가방 → 가방이

김치가 맛있어요.	The kimchi is delicious.
길이 복잡해요.	The road is crowded.
A : 가방이 싸요? B : 네, 싸요.	Is the bag cheap? Yes, it is cheap.

6. 그리고

'그리고' is used to link two sentences on an equal basis.

A : 오늘 뭐 해요? What are you doing today? B : 한국어를 공부해요. 그리고 친구를 만나요. I'm studying Korean. And I'm meeting a friend.
김치가 싸요. 그리고 맛있어요. Kimchi is cheap. And it's tasty.

UNIT 6 Time

1. ___ 시 ___ 분

When telling time, use the number system of '한, 두, 세, 네, …' for the hours, and use '일, 이, 삼, 사, …' for the minutes.

한 두 세 네 다섯 여섯 일곱 여덟 아홉 열 열한 열두	시	오 십 십오 이십 이십오 삼십 삼십오 사십 사십오 오십 오십오	분

Another expression for '삼십 분(30 minutes)' is '반(half)'.

(6 : 30) 여섯 시 삼십 분 = 여섯 시 반

A : 몇 시예요? B : 한 시 이십 분이에요.	What time is it? It's one twenty.
A : 지금 몇 시예요? B : 여섯 시 반이에요.	What time is it now? It's six thirty.

2. 요일

Days of the week in Korean

월요일 - Monday
화요일 - Tuesday
수요일 - Wednesday
목요일 - Thursday
금요일 - Friday
토요일 - Saturday
일요일 - Sunday

오늘은 월요일이에요.	Today is Monday.
A : 내일은 무슨 요일이에요? B : 화요일이에요.	What day is it tomorrow? It's Tuesday.

3. N에

The Particle '에' follows nouns which indicate time.
토요일에, 열 시에, 오 분에, 주말에, 오전에, 오후에, …
'에' is not used after '어제, 오늘, 내일'.

오늘에 친구를 만나요. (X)
→ 오늘 친구를 만나요. (O)

A : 몇 시에 밥을 먹어요?
What time do you eat your meal?
B : 8시에 먹어요.
I eat at 8 o'clock.

A : 무슨 요일에 애니 씨를 만나요?
On what day are you going to meet Annie?
B : 토요일에 만나요.
I'm going to meet her on Saturday.

A : 언제 학교에 가요?
When do you go to school?
B : 월요일하고 목요일에 가요.
I go to school on Mondays and Thursdays.

4. S-지만 S'

When two sentences show contrast in content, they can be connected by adding '-지만' to the stem of the verb or adjective of the preceding sentence.

나는 학교에 가요. 친구는 학교에 안 가요.
→ 나는 학교에 가지만 친구는 학교에 안 가요.

When two sentences are thus connected, the repeated part of the second sentence is usually omitted.

나는 학교에 가지만 친구는 학교에 안 가요.
→ 나는 학교에 가지만 친구는 안 가요.

나는 학교에 가지만 친구는 안 가요.
I go to school but my friend does not.

불고기는 맛있지만 비싸요.
Bulgogi is tasty but expensive.

UNIT 7 Appointment

1. V-(으)ㄹ까요?

'-(으)ㄹ까요?' is used for suggestions.

If the verb stem ends with a vowel + -ㄹ까요? :
가다 → 갈까요?
If the verb stem ends with a consonant + -을까요? :
먹다 → 먹을까요?

As an answer to this pattern, 'V-아요/어요' can be used. In this case, 'V-아요/어요' has the meaning 'Let's~.'

A : 뭘 먹을까요?	What shall we eat?
B : 비빔밥을 먹어요.	Let's eat bibimbap.
A : 어디에 갈까요?	Where shall we go?
B : 산에 가요.	Let's go to the mountain.

2. __ 월 __ 일

In Korean, when telling dates, the month comes first and then the date follows. For dates, we use the number system '일, 이, 삼, 사,…', therefore, when saying the month, they will be '일월, 이월, 삼월, 사월' and so on, and when saying the dates '일 일, 이 일, 삼 일, 사 일' and so on. But there are spelling changes for '6월' and '10월', which become '유월' and '시월', respectively. When asking the date, '며칠' is used.

월

Jan.	Feb.	Mar.	Apr.	May.	Jun.
일월	이월	삼월	사월	오월	유월
Jul.	Aug.	Sep.	Oct.	Nov.	Dec.
칠월	팔월	구월	시월	십일월	십이월

일

10월
시월

					1 일	2 이
3 삼	4 사	5 오	6 육	7 칠	8 팔	9 구
10 십	11 십일	12 십이	13 십삼	14 십사	15 십오	16 십육

...

오늘은 구월 이십육 일이에요.	Today is September 26.
제 생일은 삼월 십일 일이에요.	My birthday is March 11.

'며칠' is used only when asking the date, but '언제' is used generally when asking the time such as date, day, and so on. Therefore, when asking the date, '언제' can be used instead of '며칠'.

추석이 언제예요? = 추석이 며칠이에요?
시험이 언제예요? = 시험이 며칠이에요?

3. A/V-았어요/었어요

Adding '-았어요/었어요' to the stem of a verb or an adjective makes it past tense.

If the verb or adjective stem's last vowel ends with 'ㅏ' or 'ㅗ' + -았어요 : 가다 → 갔어요
If the verb or adjective ends with '하다', 하다 → 했어요 : 공부하다 → 공부했어요
In all other cases, add '-었어요' : 가르치다 → 가르쳤어요

-았어요
가다 → 갔어요
보다 → 봤어요
만나다 → 만났어요
오다 → 왔어요
좋다 → 좋았어요

-했어요
공부하다 → 공부했어요
숙제하다 → 숙제했어요
수영하다 → 수영했어요
운동하다 → 운동했어요
사랑하다 → 사랑했어요

-었어요
가르치다 → 가르쳤어요
배우다 → 배웠어요
먹다 → 먹었어요
읽다 → 읽었어요
마시다 → 마셨어요

A : 어제 뭘 했어요?
What did you do yesterday?
B : 저는 어제 친구를 만났어요.
I met a friend yesterday.

A : 마이클 씨는 어제 뭘 했어요?
What did Michael do yesterday?
B : 마이클 씨는 중국어를 공부했어요.
Michael studied Chinese.

A : 재민 씨는 어제 뭘 했어요?
What did Jaemin do yesterday?
B : 재민 씨는 산에 갔어요.
Jaemin went hiking.

4. N에서

'에서' is a particle that indicates the place where the action of the verb phrase takes place.

A : 어디에서 점심을 먹어요? B : 식당에서 먹어요.	Where do you eat lunch? I eat at the restaurant.
A : 어디에서 운동했어요? B : 공원에서 운동했어요.	Where did you exercise? I exercised at the park.

UNIT 8 Locations & Directions

1. N이/가 N'에 있다/없다

'N이/가 있어요' means that N is located or exists, 'N이/가 없어요' means the opposite. 'N'에' is used with 'N이/가 있어요' to show where N is located.

옷장이 방에 있어요.

옷장이 방에 없어요.

컴퓨터가 방에 있어요. The computer is in the room.
옷장이 방에 없어요. The closet is not in the room.

A change in word order doesn't make any change in the meaning.

옷장이 방에 있어요. = 방에 옷장이 있어요.

In this pattern, 'N이/가' can be replaced with 'N은/는'. Especially when you use this pattern consecutively, 'N은/는' sounds more natural after the first time.

A : 은행이 어디에 있어요?	Where is the bank?
B : 1층에 있어요.	It is on the first floor.
A : 화장실은 어디에 있어요?	Where is the rest room?
B : 2층에 있어요.	It is on the second floor.
A : 커피숍은 어디에 있어요?	Where is the coffee shop?
⋮	

2. N 위/아래/앞/뒤/옆/안에

Words that denote position such as '위, 아래, 앞, …' come after the noun that become the basis for the direction.

위 의자 (X) → 의자 위 (O)

의자 위

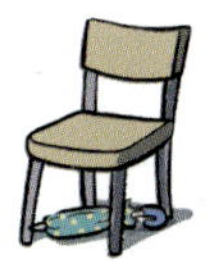

의자 아래

의자 앞

의자 뒤

의자 옆/왼쪽

의자 옆/오른쪽

가방 안

우산이 의자 위에 있어요. The umbrella is on the chair.
우산이 의자 아래에 있어요. The umbrella is under the chair.
우산이 의자 앞에 있어요. The umbrella is in front of the chair.
우산이 의자 뒤에 있어요. The umbrella is behind the chair.
우산이 의자 옆에 있어요. The umbrella is beside the chair.
우산이 가방 안에 있어요. The umbrella is inside the bag.

3. N(으)로 가다/오다

Used after a place noun, '(으)로' indicates the direction toward that place.

If the noun ends with a vowel +로 :
서울대학교 → 서울대학교로
If the noun ends with a consonant + 으로 :
앞 → 앞으로
If the noun ends with 'ㄹ'+'로' :
교실 → 교실로, 호텔 → 호텔로

이 버스는 서울대학교로 가요. This bus goes to Seoul National University.
다섯 시에 집으로 왔어요. I came home at 5 o'clock.
교실로 갈까요? Shall we go to the classroom?
앞으로 오세요. Please come to the front.

When used with specific places such as '서울대학교, 집, 교실', there is little difference between 'N(으)로 가다/오다' and 'N에 가다/오다'. But for the nouns which simply show general directions such as '앞, 뒤, 옆, 왼쪽, 오른쪽,…', only the 'N(으)로 가다/오다' pattern can be used.

집으로 가요. (O) 집에 가요. (O)
앞으로 오세요. (O) 앞에 오세요. (X)

4. N까지

'까지' after a place noun means 'until the end of a certain range.'

지하철역까지 십 분 걸려요. It takes 10 minutes to the subway station.
제주도까지 얼마나 걸려요? How long does it take to Jeju Island?

'까지' is usually used with '에서' which denotes the starting point.

집에서 학교까지 한 시간 걸려요. It takes one hour from home to school.

5. 분, 시간

When talking about the time to do something, use '분' for minutes and '시간' for hours.

5 minutes → 오 분
10 minutes → 십 분
30 minutes → 삼십 분
⋮
one hour → 한 시간
two hours → 두 시간

여기에서 학교까지 한 시간 삼십 분 걸려요. It takes one and a half hours from here to school.

UNIT 9 Phone Call

1. N-(이)지요?

'-(이)지요?' expresses either a) the speaker's strong conviction about a certain fact or state of affairs or b) that the fact or state of affairs referred to is something already known to both the speaker and listener.
When answering, the 'N-이에요/예요' pattern is used.

If the noun ends with a vowel + –지요? :
의사 → 의사지요?
If the noun ends with a consonant + –이지요? :
목요일 → 목요일이지요?

'–지요' can be abbreviated to '–죠'.
시계지요? → 시계죠?
집이지요? → 집이죠?

A : 다니엘 씨는 의사지요?
Daniel is a doctor, isn't he?
B : 네, 의사예요.
Yes, he is a doctor.

A : 오늘이 목요일이지요?
Today is Thursday, isn't it?
B : 네, 목요일이에요.
Yes, it is Thursday.

A/V–지요?

'–지요?' can come after verbs and adjectives as well. '–지요?' is added after the stem of a verb or an adjective.

A : 요즘 꽃이 비싸지요?
Flowers are expensive these days, aren't they?
B : 네, 비싸요.
Yes, they're expensive.

A : 커피를 좋아하지요?
You like coffee, don't you?
B : 네, 좋아해요.
Yes, I do.

2. V–아/어 주세요

'–아/어 주세요' is a polite form of requesting for help, assistance, etc.
'–아/어 주세요' has a meaning that the requested action is beneficial to the speaker or the receiver of the act.

If the verb stem's last vowel ends with 'ㅏ' or 'ㅗ' + –아 주세요 : 오다 → 와 주세요
If the verb ends with '하다', 하다 → 해 주세요 :
전화하다 → 전화해 주세요
In all other cases, add '–어 주세요' :
바꾸다 → 바꿔 주세요

–아 주세요	사다 → 사 주세요 오다 → 와 주세요 닫다 → 닫아 주세요
–해 주세요	전화하다 → 전화해 주세요 노래하다 → 노래해 주세요 준비하다 → 준비해 주세요
–어 주세요	바꾸다 → 바꿔 주세요 만들다 → 만들어 주세요 열다 → 열어 주세요

빨리 와 주세요.
Please come quickly.

오늘 저녁에 전화해 주세요.
Please give me a call tonight.

마이클 씨 좀 바꿔 주세요.
Can I talk to Michael, please?

3. V–고 있다

Adding '–고 있다' to a verb stem shows the action is in progress.
자다 → 자고 있어요

When negating, '안' is added in front of 'V–고 있다'.
안 자고 있어요.

크리스 씨는 공부하고 있어요.
Chris is studying.

A : 지금 뭐 하고 있어요?
What are you doing now?
B : 책을 읽고 있어요.
I'm reading a book.

Listening Transcript 듣기 지문

UNIT 1 Hangeul

p. 21

Hangeul (1)

1. 1) 아 2) 여 3) 오 4) 유 5) 으

2. 1) 이 2) 우유 3) 오이 4) 유아 5) 여유

Hangeul (2)

1. 1) 가 2) 나 3) 라 4) 바 5) 사

2. 1) 아기 2) 그리기 3) 허리 4) 두부 5) 노루

Hangeul (3)

1. 1) 까 2) 타 3) 빠 4) 차 5) 싸

2. 1) 짜다 2) 까치 3) 피다 4) 투수 5) 아빠

3. 1) 꼬마 2) 코 3) 고리 4) 도마 5) 또 6) 토끼
7) 포도 8) 바보 9) 빠르다 10) 씨 11) 소

Hangeul (4)

1. 1) 애 2) 얘 3) 와 4) 워 5) 의

2. 1) 개다 2) 위 3) 왜 4) 쇠고기 5) 의자

Hangeul (5)

1. 1) 안 2) 감 3) 속 4) 집 5) 돌

2. 1) 옷 2) 공 3) 문 4) 삽 5) 죽

3. 1) 산 2) 강 3) 밑 4) 벽 5) 발 6) 숲 7) 봄

UNIT 2 Greetings & Introductions

p. 46

1. Listen carefully, and choose the correct picture.

1) 저는 회사원이에요.

2) 베라 씨는 러시아 사람이에요.

2. Listen carefully, and choose the picture that best fits the dialogue.

마이클 : 안녕히 계세요.
여자 : 안녕히 가세요, 마이클 씨.

3. Listen carefully, and match the person with the correct nationality.

재민 : 제니 씨, 이분은 앤디 씨예요.
앤디 : 앤디예요. 반가워요.
제니 : 제니예요. 반가워요.
앤디 씨는 미국 사람이에요?
앤디 : 아니요, 캐나다 사람이에요.
제니 씨는요?
제니 : 미국 사람이에요.

4. Listen carefully, and match the person with the correct occupation.

제니 : 앤디 씨는 학생이에요?
앤디 : 아니요, 회사원이에요.
제니 씨는 선생님이에요?
제니 : 네, 저는 영어 선생님이에요.

UNIT 3 Restaurant

p. 58

1. Listen carefully, and write down the number of things that were ordered.

1) Clerk : 뭐 드릴까요?
Customer : 햄버거 두 개 주세요.

2) Clerk : 뭐 드릴까요?
Customer : 오렌지 주스 세 잔 주세요.

3) Clerk : 뭐 드릴까요?
Customer : 커피 한 잔 주세요.

4) Clerk : 뭐 드릴까요?
Customer : 맥주 다섯 병 주세요.

2. Listen carefully, and choose the correct picture that shows the items that were ordered.

1) Clerk : 뭐 드릴까요?
Customer : 오렌지 다섯 개하고 사과 두 개 주세요.

2) Clerk : 뭐 드릴까요?
Customer : 불고기 둘하고 콜라 한 병 주세요.

3) Clerk : 뭐 드릴까요?
Customer : 콜라 한 병하고 커피 네 잔 주세요.

3. Listen to the sentences, and match each sentence with the correct picture.

1) 물 좀 주세요.

2) 쓰세요.

3) 읽으세요.

4) 앉으세요.

UNIT 4 Shopping

p. 70

1. Listen carefully, and mark O if the clerk has the item in question, and mark X if he doesn't.

1) Customer : 우산이 있어요?
Clerk : 네, 있어요.

2) Customer : 시계 있어요?
Clerk : 아니요, 없어요.

3) Customer : 가방 있어요?
Clerk : 네, 가방이 있어요.

2. Listen carefully, and choose the correct price.

1) Customer : 이거 얼마예요?
Clerk : 그 가방은 삼만 원이에요.

2) Customer : 이 사과 한 개에 얼마예요?
Clerk : 그거는 하나에 이천 원이에요.

3) Customer : 저 바지는 얼마예요?
Clerk : 저거는 오만 원이에요.

3. Listen to the dialogue, and choose the correct items purchased.

1) Customer : 아저씨, 이거 얼마예요?
Clerk : 삼만 원이에요.
Customer : 삼만 원요? 너무 비싸요. 저 모자는 얼마예요?
Clerk : 이만 원이에요.
Customer : 그럼 저 모자 주세요.
Clerk : 여기요.

2) Customer : 신문 있어요?
Clerk : 아니요, 없어요.
Customer : 그럼 담배 있어요?
Clerk : 네, 있어요.
Customer : 얼마예요?
Clerk : 이천오백 원이에요.
Customer : 여기 있어요.

3) Customer : 이 사과 한 개에 얼마예요?
Clerk : 천 원이에요.
Customer : 오렌지는 얼마예요?
Clerk : 오렌지는 오백 원이에요.
Customer : 그럼 사과 두 개하고 오렌지 두 개 주세요. 모두 얼마예요?
Clerk : 삼천 원이에요.

남자 : 애니 씨는요?
애니 : 시장에 가요. 옷을 사요.
남자 : 레이 씨는요?
레이 : 공원에 가요. 운동을 해요.
남자 : 미사코 씨도 운동을 해요?
미사코 : 아니요, 저는 운동을 안 해요. 한국어를 배워요.

UNIT 5 Daily Life

p. 84

1. Listen carefully, and choose all the activities Jaemin is doing today.

여자 : 재민 씨, 오늘 학교에 가요?
재민 : 아니요, 안 가요.
여자 : 그럼 뭐 해요?
재민 : 시장에 가요.
여자 : 옷을 사요?
재민 : 아니요, 구두를 사요. 그리고 친구를 만나요.

2. Listen carefully, and mark O if Annie likes the food, and mark X if she doesn't.

남자 : 애니 씨, 불고기 좋아해요?
애니 : 네, 좋아해요.
남자 : 비빔밥은요?
애니 : 아주 좋아해요.
남자 : 나도 비빔밥을 좋아해요. 그럼 김밥은요?
애니 : 김밥은 안 먹어요.
남자 : 그럼 냉면은 먹어요?
애니 : 네. 냉면은 정말 맛있어요.

3. Connect the name of each person with the correct picture.

남자 : 리디아 씨, 오늘 뭐 해요?
리디아 : 학교에 가요. 책을 읽어요.

UNIT 6 Time

p. 98

1. Listen to the following, and fill in the blanks.

1) 남자 : 몇 시에 일어나요?
여자 : 6시 20분에 일어나요.

2) 남자 : 몇 시에 영어를 가르쳐요?
여자 : 2시 45분에 영어를 가르쳐요.

3) 남자 : 몇 시에 친구를 만나요?
여자 : 4시 반에 친구를 만나요.

4) 남자 : 몇 시에 영화를 봐요?
여자 : 9시 25분에 영화를 봐요.

2. Listen carefully, and match the time with the correct activity.

나는 5시 40분에 일어나요.
8시 20분쯤에 학교에 가요.
그리고 한국어를 공부해요.
7시 30분에 집에 가요.
그리고 11시쯤에 자요.

3. Listen carefully, and write down the number of the activity scheduled for each day.

여자 : 월요일에 뭐 해요?
남자 : 한국어를 공부해요.

여자 : 토요일에 뭐 해요?
남자 : 친구를 만나요.
여자 : 수요일에 뭐 해요?
남자 : 영화를 봐요.
여자 : 목요일에 뭐 해요?
남자 : 태권도를 배워요.

4. Listen carefully, and complete the person's schedule.

남자 : 토요일에 뭐 해요?
여자 : 병원에 가요.
남자 : 몇 시에 가요?
여자 : 오전 9시에 가요.
남자 : 일요일에도 병원에 가요?
여자 : 아니요, 토요일에는 병원에 가지만 일요일에는 안 가요.
남자 : 그럼 일요일에는 뭐 해요?
여자 : 크리스 씨를 만나요. 그리고 영화를 봐요.
남자 : 몇 시에 크리스 씨를 만나요?
여자 : 오후 3시에 만나요.

UNIT 7 Appointment

p. 111

1. Listen carefully, and write down the correct date.

1) 남자 : 오늘이 며칠이에요?
여자 : 11월 20일이에요.

2) 남자 : 오늘이 며칠이에요?
여자 : 10월 15일이에요.

3) 남자 : 생일이 언제예요?
여자 : 제 생일은 9월 13일이에요.

4) 남자 : 생일이 언제예요?
여자 : 2월 8일이에요.

5) 남자 : 언제 한국에 왔어요?
여자 : 저는 6월 4일에 왔어요.

6) 남자 : 언제 미국에 가요?
여자 : 8월 27일에 가요.

2. Listen carefully, and connect each picture with the correct date.

1) 여자 : 오늘은 뭐 해요?
남자 : 오늘은 태권도를 배워요.

2) 여자 : 언제 병원에 갔어요?
남자 : 5월 15일에 갔어요.

3) 여자 : 애니 씨 생일이 언제예요?
남자 : 5월 30일이에요.

4) 여자 : 어제 뭘 했어요?
남자 : 친구를 만났어요.

5) 여자 : 5월 7일에 뭐 했어요?
남자 : 산에 갔어요.

6) 여자 : 언제 영화를 볼까요?
남자 : 23일에 봐요.

3. Circle the correct answer.

남자 : 미사코 씨, 토요일에 영화 볼까요?
미사코 : 토요일은 바빠요.
남자 : 그럼 일요일은 어때요?
미사코 : 일요일은 좋아요.
남자 : 영화 '친구'를 볼까요?
미사코 : 그 영화는 봤어요. 영화 '집으로'는 어때요?
남자 : 좋아요. '집으로'를 봐요.
그럼 일요일에 어디에서 만날까요?
미사코 : 2시에 한국극장 앞에서 만나요.
남자 : 좋아요.

Listening Transcript 듣기 지문

UNIT 8 Locations & Directions

p. 125

1. Listen carefully, and connect each picture with the correct floor of the department store.

1) Customer : 구두가 몇 층에 있어요?
Clerk : 4층에 있어요.

2) Customer : 가방은 어디에 있어요?
Clerk : 1층에 있어요.

3) Customer : 바지는 2층에 있어요?
Clerk : 네, 2층에 있어요.

4) Customer : 책은 5층에 있어요?
Clerk : 아니요, 7층에 있어요.

5) Customer : 식당은 어디에 있어요?
Clerk : 9층에 있어요.

6) Customer : 커피숍은 어디에 있어요?
Clerk : 식당 옆에 있어요.

2. Listen to the dialogue, and write down the number of the place where the following item is located.

1) 여자 : 가방이 어디에 있어요?
남자 : 책상 옆에 있어요.

2) 여자 : 우산은 책상 위에 있어요?
남자 : 네, 책상 위에 있어요.

3) 여자 : 신문은 어디에 있어요?
남자 : 의자 아래에 있어요.

4) 여자 : 코트는 옷장 안에 있어요?
남자 : 아니요, 침대 위에 있어요.

3. Listen to the dialogue, and write down the number of each building the person is looking for.

1) 여자 : 이 근처에 우체국이 있어요?
남자 : 네, 있어요. 이쪽으로 백 미터쯤 가세요.
우체국은 세탁소 옆에 있어요.

2) 여자 : 저, 병원이 어디에 있어요?
남자 : 약국 뒤에 있어요.
여자 : 감사합니다.

3) 여자 : 서울은행이 어디에 있어요?
남자 : 이쪽으로 쭉 가세요. 그럼 왼쪽에 약국이 있어요.
서울은행은 약국 옆에 있어요.
여자 : 네, 고맙습니다.

UNIT 9 Phone Call

p. 138

1. Listen to the dialogue carefully. If the caller made the right call, mark O, and if the caller made the wrong call, mark X.

1) 여자1 : 여보세요. 재민 씨 집이지요?
여자2 : 네, 그런데요.

2) 웨이 : 여보세요. 거기 크리스 씨 집이지요?
크리스 : 네, 전데요. 실례지만 누구세요?
웨이 : 저 웨이예요.

3) 남자 : 여보세요. 거기 서울대학교지요?
여자 : 아닌데요.

2. Saturday is Annie's birthday. Jaemin is organizing a party for Annie. Listen carefully, and match each person with the thing he/she should prepare.

1) 재민 : 웨이 씨, 이번 토요일에 애니 씨 생일 파티를 해요.
웨이 씨는 케이크를 만들어 주세요.
웨이 : 좋아요.

2) 재민 : 여보세요. 크리스 씨?
크리스 : 네, 전데요.
재민 : 토요일에 애니 씨 생일 파티를 해요.
크리스 씨는 생일 파티 노래를 준비해 주세요.

3) 재민 : 알렉스 씨, 이번 토요일에 시간 있어요?
알렉스 : 네, 있어요.

재민　: 토요일에 애니 씨 생일 파티가 있어요.
알렉스 씨는 꽃을 준비해 주세요.

4) 재민　: 미사코 씨, 저 재민인데요.
토요일에 애니 씨 생일 파티에 오지요?
미사코 : 네.
재민　: 그럼 미사코 씨는 일본 음식을 만들어 주세요.
미사코 : 네, 알겠어요.

3. Listen to the dialogue, and mark O if it is correct, and mark X if it is incorrect.

크리스 : 여보세요. 거기 재민 씨 집이지요?
여자　: 네, 그런데요.
크리스 : 안녕하세요? 저는 친구 크리스예요. 재민 씨 집에 있어요?
여자　: 지금 집에 없어요. 도서관에서 공부하고 있어요.
크리스 : 네, 알겠습니다. 안녕히 계세요.

Glossary 찾아보기

ㄱ

		Unit
가게	store / shop	8
가다	to go	3
가르치다	to teach	5
가방	bag	4
가위바위보	rock, paper, scissors	9
개	counting unit for general items	3
걸리다	to take (time)	8
고기	meat	5
공부	study / learning	5
공부하다	to study	5
공원	park	5
공책	notebook	4
과일	fruit	8
교실	classroom	8
구	nine	4
구두	dress shoes	4
구월	September	7
국적	nationality	2
그	that	4
그거	that (one)	4
그럼	then / in that case	4
그리고	and	5
그리다	to draw / to paint	9
그림	picture / drawing	9
극장	movie theater	7
금요일	Friday	6
기다리다	to wait	3
기자	reporter	2
길	road / way	5
김밥	gimbap	3
김치	kimchi	3

ㄴ

		Unit
나	I	6
날씨	weather	5
내일	tomorrow	5
냉면	naengmyeon	3
냉장고	refrigerator	8
네	four (when modifying a counting unit that follows)	3
넷	four	3
노래하다	to sing	9
녹차	green tea	3

ㄷ

		Unit
다섯	five	3
닫다	to close	9
담배	cigarette	4
더	more	3
도서관	library	7
독일	Germany	2
돈	money	4
두	two (when modifying a counting unit that follows)	3
둘	two	3
뒤	behind	8
따뜻하다	warm	5

ㄹ

		Unit
라면	ramen	3
러시아	Russia	2

ㅁ

		Unit
마시다	to drink	5
만	ten thousand	4
만나다	to meet	5
만들다	to make	9
맛있다	tasty / delicious	5
맥주	beer	3
먹다	to eat	5
메뉴	menu	3
며칠	what date	7
몇	how many	3
모자	hat / cap	4
목요일	Thursday	6
무슨	what kind of	6
문	door	9
물	water	3
뭐	what	4
뭘	what	5
미국	the United States of America	2

ㅂ

		Unit
바꾸다	to change	9
바나나	banana	5
바지	trousers / pants	4
반	half	6
받다	to receive / to take / to get	9
밥	steamed rice	5
방	room	8
배우다	to learn	5
백	hundred	4
백화점	department store	6
버스	bus	8
병	counting unit for bottles	3
병원	hospital	5
보다	to see / to watch	5
복잡하다	crowded / jammed	5
볼펜	ball-point pen	4
부엌	kitchen	9
분	minute(s)	6
불고기	bulgogi	3
비빔밥	bibimbap	3
비싸다	expensive	6
빨래하다	to do laundry	5
빨리	quickly	9
빵	bread	3

ㅅ

		Unit
사	four	4
사과	apple	3
사다	to buy	5
사람	person	2
사월	April	7
사전	dictionary	4
산	mountain	5
삼	three	4
삼월	March	7
생선	fish	8
생일	birthday	7
샤워하다	to take a shower	6
서울대학교	Seoul National University	8

Glossary 찾아보기

| ㅇ |

우산 umbrella 4
우유 milk 3
우체국 post office 8
운동 exercise / workout 5
운동하다 to exercise / to work out 5
원 KRW / won (Korean money) 4
월 month 7
월요일 Monday 6
위 above / on 8
유월 June 7
육 six 4
은행 bank 8
은행원 bank clerk 2
음식 food 9
의사 doctor 2
의자 chair 8
이 this 4
이 two 4
이거 this (one) 4
이름 name 2
이분 this person (honorific) 2
이월 February 7
인도 India 2
일 day 7
일 one 4
일곱 seven 3
일본 Japan 2
일본어 Japanese (language) 7
일어나다 to get up 6
일요일 Sunday 6
일월 January 7
일하다 to work 6
읽다 to read 3
입다 to wear / to put on 5
있다 to have 4

| ㅈ |

Unit

자다 to sleep 6
잔 counting unit for glasses or cups 3
재미있다 interesting 5
저 I 2
저 that 4
저거 that (one) 4
저녁 evening 9
전화 telephone 2
전화하다 to call 9
점심 lunch 7
제 my 4
좀 please 3
좋다 good 5
좋아하다 to like 5
주다 to give 3
주말 weekend 6
주소 address 2
주스 juice 3
준비하다 to prepare 9
중국 China 2
지금 now 5
지하철역 subway station 8
직업 job / occupation 2
질문 question 5
집 house 5
쯤 about / around 6

| ㅊ |

Unit

창문 window 9
책 book 4
책방 bookstore 7
책상 desk 8

Glossary 찾아보기

		Unit
천	thousand	4
청소하다	to clean	5
추석	the Korean Thanksgiving	7
춤추다	to dance	9
층	floor	8
치마	skirt	4
친구	friend	5
칠	seven	4
칠월	July	7
침대	bed	8

ㅋ

		Unit
카메라	camera	4
캐나다	Canada	2
커피	coffee	3
커피숍	coffee shop	7
컴퓨터	computer	8
케이크	cake	9
코트	coat	8
콜라	cola	3

ㅌ

		Unit
태권도	taekwondo	5
텔레비전	television	5
토요일	Saturday	6

ㅍ

		Unit
파티	party	7
팔	eight	4
팔월	August	7
포도	grape(s)	5
프랑스	France	2
피자	pizza	5

ㅎ

		Unit
하나	one	3
하다	to do	5
학교	school	5
학생	student	2
한	one (when modifying a counting unit that follows)	3
한국	Korea	2
한국어	Korean (language)	4
햄버거	hamburger	3
호주	Australia	2
호텔	hotel	8
홍차	black tea	3
화요일	Tuesday	6
화장실	rest room	8
회사원	company employee	2
회의하다	to hold a meeting	9
휴대 전화	cellular phone/mobile	4

집필위원

최은규 서울대학교 국어국문학과 박사
서울대학교 언어교육원 한국어교육센터 대우부교수

장은아 고려대학교 교육학과 박사
서울대학교 언어교육원 한국어교육센터 대우조교수

김은아 서울대학교 외국어교육과 박사과정 수료
서울대학교 언어교육원 한국어교육센터 대우조교수

채숙희 서울대학교 국어국문학과 박사
서울시립대학교 국제교육원 객원교수

남수경 서울대학교 국어국문학과 박사
서울대학교 인문학연구원 선임연구원

이숙현 시드니대학교 인문학부 석사
전 서울대학교 언어교육원 강사
모내시 대학교 한국학과 강사

Active Korean 1

지은이 서울대학교 언어교육원
발행처 (주)투판즈
주소 서울시 강남구 논현로 303
전화 (02)2140-2500
팩스 (02)2140-2599
인터넷 주소 www.twoponds.co.kr
등록 1980년 10월 7일 제2004-000086호
초판 1쇄 2006년 8월 1일
64쇄 2026년 3월 1일

「이 도서의 국립중앙도서관 출판시도서목록(CIP)은
e-CIP 홈페이지(http://www.nl.go.kr/ecip)에서 이용하실 수 있습니다.
(CIP제어번호: CIP2006001435)」